Longmc

Teacher's Book

2

Brian Abbs • Anne Worrall • Ann Ward

Course summary

Unit	Topic	Language
1 Hi!	Meeting people	*Greetings:* Hello/Hi Good morning Goodbye/bye *Introductions:* I'm
2 How are you?	Meeting people	*Greetings:* Good afternoon How are you? I'm fine, thanks. *Identifying people:* he's/she's *Numbers:* 1 – 10.
3 What's your name?	The classroom	*Instructions:* Sit down. Stand up. Open your books. Close your books. Quiet, please. *Introductions:* This is (Jill). My name's (Ben).
4 Ben's family	The family	*Introductions:* What's your name? My/his/her name's (Mary). *Identifying people:* Is this (Jenny)? Yes./No. This is my/(Ben)'s sister.
5 What's this?	Familiar sights and sounds	*Identifying objects:* What's this? It's /It isn't a (car). Is it a (car)? *Correcting:* No, it's a (bus).
6 Is this your hat?	Clothes	*Possession:* Whose (hat) is this? It's my/your/his/her (hat). It's (Jenny)'s (hat). *Instructions:* Put on (your jacket). Take off (your shoes).
7 Happy birthday, Jill!	Celebrations	*Ages:* How old are you? I'm nine (years old). *Identifying objects:* What is it? It's a (watch).
8 Colors!	Colors	*Colors:* What color is it? It's (red). *Preferences:* My favorite color is (red). is/are
9 Our street	Local community	*Addresses:* Who lives here? (Jenny) lives here. I live at 10 Lime Avenue. *Checking information:* Is this your (house)?

Unit	Topic	Language
10 **A spider in the bathroom**	Rooms in a house Insects	*Location:* There's (a spider) in the bathroom. in/on *Plurals* *Likes/dislikes:* I like (spiders). I don't like (ants). Do you like (spiders)?
11 **I like snails**	Animals	*Likes/dislikes* *Describing a place:* There is/are/isn't … *Contradicting:* It isn't a dog. It's a horse.
12 **I like pizza**	Food	*Likes/dislikes* *Preferences:* I like apples but I don't like cheese.
13 **Where is it?**	Looking for things Furniture	*Location:* Where's my (coat)? Where are my (shoes)? It's/they're (on the couch). *Prepositions:* in/on/under/behind
14 **A safari park**	Wild animals	*Quantity:* Are there any (seals)? No, there aren't. How many (seals) are there? There are five.
15 **I'm making a robot!**	Parts of the body	*Identifying objects:* This is (his head). These are (his legs). *Present continuous:* What are you doing? I'm making a robot. *Possession:* I have/he/she has (a head).
16 **A model village!**	Buildings	*Describing a town:* There's (a station). There isn't (a school). *Checking information:* Is there (a station)? Are there any (houses)?
17 **We're going to the moon!**	Space travel	*Present continuous:* We're going to the moon. our/their have/don't have
18 **I'm standing on my head**	Doing exercises	*Present continuous:* I'm touching my toes. *Imperatives:* Lift your arms.
19 **Mary's pen pal**	Friends Nationalities	*Descriptions of people* (Review) *Numbers:* 11 – 20
20 **Smile please!**	Taking photos	Review

Introduction

1 Aims of the course

Popcorn is a new four level elementary course to help you and your pupils get the most out of English.

Popcorn uses children's creative energy as a classroom resource. The aim is to encourage children to develop language and educational skills and to enjoy the learning process. Children's natural interests are engaged and maintained through lively stories and a variety of activities, including games and songs.

Topics

The topics have been chosen for their interest and appropriateness to children of this age. Language learning is combined with general educational skills. Pupils are encouraged to talk first about themselves and their surroundings and then to broaden their horizons. **Popcorn** incorporates work from other areas of the school curriculum and offers a range of opportunities to learn about other cultures and ways of life.

Activities

Popcorn is crammed with lively activities which are designed to help children use the language they learn creatively and to apply it to their own lives.

Language

Popcorn has a realistic syllabus. New structures are introduced at a gradual pace and there is constant recycling so that pupils become familiar and confident with what they have learned.

Skills

The course gives plenty of practice in the four skills of speaking, listening, reading and writing. The Pupils' Book focuses on speaking and listening. The Activity Book focuses on reading and writing.

Cultural background

The artwork in **Popcorn** has been specially designed to reflect the cultural background in which the stories take place. Pupils are encouraged to compare this background with their own to broaden their awareness of diverse cultural identity.

2 Teaching English to children – general guidelines

Creative use of language

Allow your pupils' natural imaginative instinct to make them active learners. Children should be encouraged to use English creatively, to experiment with the language they are learning and to apply it to various situations. Games, puzzles, pairwork and groupwork encourage children to work together and to solve problems for themselves. They are therefore an essential part of the course.

Mistakes

In the course of experimenting with the language, children will make mistakes. It is important to realize that this is a natural and useful part of the learning process. Mistakes should not therefore be corrected in ways that discourage pupils from trying out new ways of using language. Too much emphasis on accuracy can be inhibiting. During a game, for example, it is not appropriate or possible to correct all mistakes as they occur. It is better to make a note of persistent mistakes and work on them later.

In many of the oral exercises, the teacher's task is to help pupils to express what they need to say rather than correct mistakes. On the other hand, some exercises, such as the written exercises in the Activity Book or the model dialogs, are designed to improve accuracy. These can be corrected and mistakes discussed in more detail.

Settling down and brightening up

You will find that different types of activities have different effects on pupils. Some activities help to settle pupils down and others make them animated.

In general, activities involving writing, drawing, reading and listening have a settling effect. Many of the Activity Book exercises fall into this category. Games, songs and some oral activities animate pupils and brighten them up after a quiet session.

It is useful to have some settling down and brightening up activities on hand so that you can vary the mood of your class. For example, a writing activity such as copying new words into their picture dictionaries will settle the class down and a game or a song will liven them up.

It may be advisable to change the order of the activities suggested in the lesson notes sometimes to fit in with your pupils' mood, e.g. if they arrive in an excitable mood and you want to help them settle down.

Use of L1

Your aim should be to use as much English as possible in the class. Introduce English classroom language from the beginning (see page 9). Help pupils to correct themselves when they say something in L1 that they should be able to say in English, e.g. *Thank you.* Try to get pupils used to the idea that certain times in the lesson are "English only" times, for example, when they are doing pairwork.

Use L1 to ask questions about the background of stories and new situations to make your pupils more interested in them. Instructions for new activities can be given in English and its L1 equivalent. Avoid explaining grammar rules: these are too difficult for young pupils to grasp and at this stage are unnecessary.

3 Organization of the course and teaching methods

The course consists of 20 units of 4 lessons each, providing material for up to 80 teaching hours, although this can be adapted to your needs.

The course contains:
- Pupils' Book
- Activity Book
- A set of two class cassettes
- The Teacher's Book

Pupils' Book

New language is introduced in a picture story at the beginning of each unit. Your pupils will follow the exploits of some American children of their own age at school and at home. The artwork has been specially designed to reflect the cultural background of the story and to grab your pupils' attention!

There are a variety of practice activities, including games, a listening exercise, pairwork, rhymes and songs. The Pupils' Book exercises focus on speaking, listening and reading.

Listening exercises are indicated by the symbol 🎛, pairwork by the symbol 😀, and personalization exercises by the symbol your turn!.

A special fun feature is the animated "flick" pictures of Mozart the dog at the top right-hand corner of each page. Let pupils discover for themselves that if they flick the book from front to back, he moves.

Activity Book

Pupils consolidate what they have learned with exercises and puzzles involving writing, listening, reading and drawing and coloring. There is a special "write a story" feature with traditional fairy story characters.

Alternate units of the Activity Book have a craft activity lesson, indicated by the symbol ✂, where pupils learn by making something and using their creative talents. The Teacher's Book gives ideas on how to use the things pupils make in the classroom, for a variety of language activities.

The Activity Book also has an animated "flick" cat.

The cassettes

The cassettes contain a recording of the story in the Pupils' Book, complete with sound effects, the listening exercises for the Pupils' Book and Activity Book, the model dialogs for pupils to use in the pairwork activities and the songs and rhymes.

The classroom language listed on pages 9 and 10 is recorded at the beginning of the cassette. It is not recommended to be played as a list for pupils.

The Teacher's Book

The Teacher's Book provides step-by-step lesson notes along with guidance for how to warm your pupils up at the beginning of the lesson and how to bring the lesson to a close.

Suggestions are also given for extension and project work which will help your pupils expand their language work to reflect broader spheres and other curriculum subjects. Not all the ideas have to be taken up. You might like to select projects which fit in with the work pupils are doing in other parts of the curriculum.

4 Guidelines on specific activities

Pupils may take some time to get used to new kinds of activities. Make sure that they fully understand what is expected of them and give a little time to allow them to feel confident doing the activity. The following guidelines suggest procedures for certain common activities.

Pairwork

Pairwork allows pupils to make maximum use of classroom time. It increases the time they spend speaking and ensures that they contribute to the class. The following steps will help you to set it up effectively:

- Make sure that pupils are familiar with all the language that they need for the activity.
- Select pairs.
- Give the instructions and make sure pupils have understood, using gestures or L1.
- Demonstrate the activity using a couple of pairs of pupils.
- Start the activity. Monitor (go round the class listening, helping and encouraging where necessary. You could also make a mental note of difficulties for further review work).

It can be more settling for pupils to work with a regular partner but it can vary the activity if you get pupils to work with new partners. Finding a new partner can be a useful language exercise in itself! You can arrange it as a game by giving each pupil half of a matching pair and asking them to find their partner, e.g. half a picture or a question and an answer, or a picture and a word.

Groupwork

When they work in groups, pupils should be able to see each other and interact, so they should be grouped around a table or with their desks pushed together. Similar steps to those for pairwork should be followed for setting up the activity.

Teaching vocabulary

Use the pictures in the book and objects in the class to teach new vocabulary. In addition to the pictures in the story, each unit has a strip of pictures at the beginning which reflects the theme of the unit and can be used for teaching vocabulary.

- Point to the picture/object and try to elicit the new word from the pupils first.
- Say the word and ask pupils to repeat.
- Write the new word on the board.
- Check they have understood by asking them to point to the correct picture/object.

Direct translation can be useful with more abstract vocabulary but should be avoided if possible.

Help your pupils to remember new words by storing them in an ordered way. In Unit 5, pupils are shown how to make a picture dictionary. New words should be added to this as they are introduced.

The story

The story material can be exploited in the following way:

- Engage children's interest by looking at the pictures and asking them about them in English or L1.
- Teach key words if they are essential to general understanding. Not all new language should be highlighted at this point though. Let the pupils hear and see it in the context of the story first.
- Play the cassette while pupils listen and follow in their books.
- Ask a few simple questions (in English or L1) to check comprehension.
- Play the cassette again for pupils to listen and repeat. Pupils will enjoy this more if they are really encouraged to "act" what they are repeating – copying the intonation and perhaps repeating the sound effects!
- Pupils can read the dialog in pairs or groups. They could also act it out in front of the class, with props if possible.

Model dialogs

Many of the Pupils' Book exercises have model dialogs on the cassette.

- Talk about the pictures in English or L1. Teach any new words.
- Play the cassette and ask pupils to repeat.
- Put the pupils into pairs.
- Ask a couple of pairs to demonstrate the dialog.
- Pairs practice together while you monitor.

Some of the dialogs can be done using the puppets made by the pupils in Unit 1. In the early stages of the course, using the puppets may help to make pupils less self-conscious.

Pupils can make up extra dialogs of their own and extra dialogs can be made using the material in the Activity Book. (These are suggested in the Lesson Notes.)

Songs and rhymes

Besides being enjoyable for the pupils, songs and rhymes are invaluable for practicing intonation and pronunciation. They can be exploited in a number of ways. Here is a standard procedure:

- Talk about the pictures in English or L1. Pupils can try to guess what the song is about. Teach any key words.

- Play the song on cassette. Pupils listen. They can start humming the tune as it becomes familiar.

- Play the song again, line by line, pausing for pupils to repeat.

- Play the song again and let pupils sing along.

- In addition, pupils can be divided into groups to sing alternate verses, asked to mime the actions of the song as they sing, even to write their own verses! Pupils will often want to hear their favorite songs again and again.

Note: Sometimes the songs contain structures and vocabulary that are more advanced than the language pupils have been learning. This is a useful way of exposing them to more language receptively. Explain the meaning of the song and of individual words, but there is no need to teach this language in a formal way.

Games

Games channel children's natural instinct for fun into successful language learning!

As with pairwork and groupwork, make sure that pupils understand the activity and demonstrate with groups of pupils first. Play the games again and again, to review language and to vary the pace of lessons. Pupils will probably enjoy some of the games more the second time they play – as they become more confident and know the rules.

Craft activities

Children will enjoy these craft activities which

encourage them to learn English as they make something.

The materials needed for each of these activities are listed in the Activity Book and in the Teacher's Book. Work out how many of each item you will need before the lesson.

If you have time, it would also be helpful to have prepared a sample of the object they are going to make (puppet, rocket, etc.) before the class. This will help you to make sure that the materials you have are suitable (the right weight of cardboard, the right type of glue, etc.) and to foresee any difficulties your pupils may experience. It is also useful to be able to show pupils what they are going to make.

- Make sure pupils understand what they have to do by demonstrating – either with the object you have made before the class, or by mime. Use English throughout – your demonstration should make the meaning clear.

- Divide pupils into groups. Make sure that each group has the necessary materials.

- Go around the class helping and encouraging where necessary.

Class surveys

Pupils often personalize the language they learn through a class survey. For example, if the topic has been pets, they will find out what the class's most popular type of pets are.

- Ask pupils to copy a chart from the board with a list of questions to ask each other and space for pupils' answers. For example:

name	Ana	Claudia	Niklas	Stefan
1 Do you have a pet?				
2 What is it?				

Pupils can suggest some of the questions.

- Make sure pupils understand what they have to do. Demonstrate with a couple of pupils.

- Pupils go around the class asking each other the questions and noting down the answers in their books.

- Pupils sort the information out and present it as a chart, bar chart, etc. Ways of presenting class survey information are suggested in the lesson notes in the Teacher's Book.

Pronunciation

Pronunciation and intonation is practiced through songs and rhymes and by listening and repeating material on the cassette.

Spelling

The written activities and puzzles in the Activity Book will help you to check pupils' spelling. Here are some other ways to make it more fun:

- Anagrams. Jumble up the letters and ask pupils to make a word: PALPE (apple). Pupils can also make up their own anagrams.

- Write words on the board with letters missing: A– – – E.

- Give out sets of alphabet cards and ask pupils to make words.

Project work

Projects encourage pupils to take an active role in exploring topics further and to relate what they are learning in their English class to other parts of the curriculum.

Pupils do not have to do all the projects suggested in the Teacher's Book. It would be best to choose those that best relate to pupils' own lives and experiences or complement the work they are doing in other lessons.

Pupils can do projects in groups, each group collecting information and material for a poster or a file on the subject.

Posters should be displayed in the class. If possible, an area of the classroom wall should be set aside for pupils' drawings and writing in English, which can be used as a teaching aid and to generate interest.

Cultural awareness

Popcorn offers children the chance to learn about life in other countries in their English lessons. The pictures in the main story show cultural aspects of American life and other exercises include photos to show cultural aspects from other countries around the world.

- Ask pupils to look at the picture/photo and tell you (L1) what things they can see that are different from things in their own country.

- Ask pupils to tell you what else they know about the country/people shown.

- Pupils can imagine what it's like to spend a day as the people in the pictures – Ben and Jill or Yoko and Stefan (in Unit 4).

- Pupils can draw pictures of similar scenes in their own countries. You can encourage pupils to make a "cultural file" with their drawings (labelled) and pictures from magazines.

5 Materials needed

We have kept extra materials needed to a minimum.

Much of the pupils' writing will be in the Activity Book. In addition to this pupils are asked to draw and write about aspects of their own lives. For this they will need colored pencils and sheets of paper. The drawings should be kept for question and answer sessions and for display in the class. They can also be kept by pupils in a loose-leaf folder, which will be more useful than a notebook.

Apart from the materials needed for the Craft Activities (see page 7) the following teaching aids would be useful:

Flashcards

These are cards you prepare with writing or pictures on. They can be used to introduce and review new language. They should be drawn/written on stiff card and be big enough for pupils to see/read when you hold them up.

Magazine pictures

Pictures from magazines can also be mounted on cardboard to be used as a visual aid. It is often difficult to find the right pictures just before you need them; cut out and keep pictures you think will be useful and save them for use later in the course. Pictures we have found useful include pictures of families doing different things in the home, animals, food, people of different ages, transportation and clothes.

Magazine pictures can also act as extra cultural background material, as can any English "realia" material – tourist brochures, labels off food, English comics, etc.

A map or a globe

Objects

Real objects or models (clothes, toy cars, etc.) often help to focus pupils' attention and can make vocabulary more meaningful to pupils.

6 Charting progress

As the course progresses, you (and parents!) will want to see how your pupils are getting on. Their performance in class will obviously give you a good idea but progress can be monitored in a number of other ways. Assessment should be approached sensitively, as it is important that pupils are not discouraged by bad results.

Assessment activities

At the end of the lesson notes for each unit in the Teacher's Book there is a suggestion for an activity which will help you to assess informally if pupils have grasped the main language points of the unit. These activities should be fitted into a normal lesson when time permits.

An assessment chart

You can make a chart to record progress. This can be filled in with numbers or with symbols:

name	Assessment 1	Assessment 2	Assessment 3
Ana	1	2	1
Claudia	2	3	2
Niklas	2	1	1

1 = very good, 2 = good, 3 = needs attention

Informal assessment

In class, you can assess pupils informally by asking extra questions to individual pupils as you go around the class while they are doing pairwork to make sure that all pupils know what is going on.

It is also worthwhile to observe the way pupils perform in pairwork or groupwork, to identify those who seem to be struggling.

Tests

There are three tests at the back of the Teacher's Book. These can be photocopied. They include a listening test (which the teacher reads), reading and writing exercises. The teacher's script for the listening test and the key to the exercises is on page 96 of the Teacher's Book.

Pupils should do these tests individually. Try to arrange the class so that they cannot see each other's work. Make sure that pupils do not feel intimidated by these tests; their main purpose is to show you which areas need further work.

Putting things right

If the assessment shows that most of the class has performed badly, repeat relevant exercises in the Pupils' Book, ask additional oral questions and practice writing sentences using the language point. Then do the assessment activity again.

If some pupils are consistently performing badly, try to give them some extra attention while they are working in class, sitting in and helping them with their pairwork. Make sure they understand new language and know what they have to do in the exercises. It sometimes helps to change their partners for pairwork.

7 Classroom language

This should be introduced gradually and naturally as it comes up in the course of your lessons. Introduce new examples of classroom language using the English first, then the L1 equivalent, if necessary. Gradually stop using the L1 equivalent as pupils learn the new language.

Greetings
Hello/Hi
Good morning.
Good morning, Miss Fisher.

Basic instructions
Watch.
Watch carefully.

Listen.
Listen carefully.

Look.
Look at this.
Look at page 10.
Look at picture 2.
Listen and look.

Point.
Point to Ben.
Point to the dog.
Point to the right picture.

Touch.
Touch your desk.
Touch something blue.
Listen and touch the right thing.

Read.
Read this word.
Read the story.
Read this page.
Read the part of Ben.
Read the words and match the
    pictures.

Draw.
Draw a picture.
Draw a picture of Elvis.
Draw a picture and color it.

Show me.
Show me something blue.
Show me your pictures.
Hold up your pictures.

Write.
Write the words.

Tell the class.
Tell me about your family.
Tell us about Ben.
Tell your friend about your
    picture.
Who can tell me the answer?
Hands up!

Organizing the class
Sit down, please.
Stand up, please.
Come here.
Work in pairs.
Work in groups.
In pairs, please.
In groups, please, everyone.
Close the door, please.
Can you close the door, please?
Open the window, please, Sally.
Take out your books.
Where's your book, Susannah?
Do you have a pencil, Jenny?
Do you all have a pencil?

Changing activities
Let's play a game.
Do you want to play a game
    now?
Start now!
Stop now!
Let's sing a song.
Who can sing this song?
Let's act this story.
You can be Jill and you can be
    Eddy.

Taking turns
Whose turn is it?
It's my turn.
It's your turn.
It's Cathy's turn.

Can I read now?
All right, Alex.

Will you read, please, Fiona?
You can read now, Jenny.
Who wants to read now?

Can I go to the bathroom, please?
OK. Be quick.

Quickly and quietly
Quickly, everyone.
Come on, James.
Sh! Quiet!
Keep quiet, please.
Quietly, please.
Don't do that, Catherine!

Questions about language
What's this in English?
It's "cat".

How do you spell it?
C–A–T.

Who can spell "banana" in
    English?
Me!

How do you say "pizza" in
    English?
You say "pizza"!

Praise
Good!
That's good!
Very good!
What a nice picture!
That's very good!
Almost right, Ann, try again.

Activity lessons
Cut.
Cut out the squares.

Glue.
Glue the squares together.

Make.
Make a robot.

Some scissors, some glue, some
    paper, some string.
I need a piece of paper.
I need some glue.

Finishing up
Time to stop now.
Collect the books, Jack.
Put your books away.

Who can be ready first?

At the end of the lesson
See you tomorrow.
See you on Monday.
Goodbye, everyone.
Bye bye.

Unit 1 Hi!

Background information

In the story, Ben is going to school. On the way, he meets his friends Tom and Jenny, Mr. Hill the crossing guard, and Mr. Cooper the mailman. When he arrives at school, he meets Miss Fisher, his teacher. Ben is late for school.

A crossing guard stops the traffic where children have to cross the road on the way to and from school.

Ben greets his friends with the less formal "Hi" and the adults with "Good morning".

Lesson 1

Language	New words and expressions
*Mr./Miss	hello hi
*I'm	good morning
	thank you
	and

* = *new language*

Beginning the lesson

- Open Pupils' Books at page 2 and discuss the story in L1. Point out the characters in the story using the motif strip at the side of the page: Ben, Tom, Jenny, Mr. Hill, Mr. Cooper and Miss Fisher. Ask questions about the story, encouraging pupils to guess if necessary. Where is Ben going? Is he in a hurry? Why? Who is Mr. Cooper? Who is Miss Fisher? What do you think Mr. Hill is doing? Explain Mr. Hill's job. What do you think Ben is saying to his friends? Do you think it is morning or afternoon in the story?

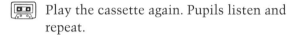 **Hi!**

Listen and look.

 Listen to the cassette together. Pupils follow the text in the Pupils' Book.

- Say the names of the characters: *Ben, Tom, Jenny, Mr. Hill, Mr. Cooper,* and *Miss Fisher,* as pupils point to them in the pictures.

- Explain that *Good morning* is a more formal greeting than *Hello. Hi* is more informal than *Hello,* and it is more common for children to greet each other like this. Ask pupils in L1 to find out to whom Ben says *Good morning* and to whom he says *Hi.*

 Play the cassette again. Pupils listen and repeat.

- Practice saying *Good morning* and *Hello/Hi* to the whole class: *Good morning.* (*Good morning, Miss/Mr. ...*).

PB 4 ex 1 | **I'm Ben**

Listen and point.

- Introduce *I'm.* Point to yourself and say *I'm ....* Tell pupils that they are going to hear the people in the pictures speaking. Pupils point to each person when they hear him or her speaking.

 Play the cassette. Pupils listen and point.

Tapescript and key

I'm Ben. (1)
I'm Miss Fisher. (3)
I'm Mr. Hill. (4)
I'm Jenny. (5)
I'm Tom. (2)

AB 2 ex A | **Match the names and the pictures. Draw a line.**

- Pupils work in pairs or on their own matching the names and the pictures with a line.

- Read the sentences aloud: *I'm Ben,* etc. Pupils listen and point.

- Pupils say their own names: *I'm ..., Hello, I'm ... .*

Ending the lesson

 Listen to the story again on cassette.

- Pupils can draw one of the people from the story and write his or her name: *Hi, I'm Tom*.

Lesson 2

Language	New words and expressions
Hello, I'm (Ben). Good morning, I'm (Miss Fisher).	goodbye

Beginning the lesson

- Greet pupils: *Good morning. (Good morning, Miss/Mr. ...)*. In L1, ask pupils to tell the class their names in English: *Hello, I'm ... .*

- Ask pupils in L1 to tell you what is happening in the picture story. Ask them to tell you who the characters are and then find and point to the words *Hello, Hi* and *Good morning*.

PB 4 ex 2 **Who are they?**

Read and match.

- Ask pupils to look at the pictures of the puppets and guess which of the characters in the story on pages 2 and 3 of the Pupils' Book they represent.

- Pupils read in pairs, finding and pointing to the people in the pictures. Go around the class, helping pupils to read the sentences.

- Check the answers. Read each sentence aloud. Pupils find the people and point to their pictures.

 Pupils practice saying *Hi, I'm ...* and *Good morning, I'm ...* in pairs, using their own names.

PB 5 ex 3 **Hello and goodbye**

What are they saying? Listen and point.

- Introduce *Goodbye*. Look at the pictures and tell pupils that some of the people are saying *Hello* or *Hi* and others are saying *Goodbye* or *Bye*. Ask a pupil to point to someone in the pictures saying *Goodbye*.

 Play the cassette. Pupils listen and point to the correct picture. Pause the cassette and check after each section.

Tapescript and key

Tom:	Hi, Mr. Hill.
Mr. Hill:	Good morning, Tom. (2)
Jenny:	Ben! Hi!
Ben:	Hi, Jenny! Hi, Tom! (5)
Miss Fisher:	Goodbye, Jenny.
Jenny:	Goodbye, Miss Fisher. (1)
Mr. Hill:	Good morning, Jenny!
Jenny:	Hello, Mr. Hill. (4)
Tom:	Bye, Jenny!
Jenny:	Goodbye, Tom. (3)

Divide the class into two groups. Tell one group to be Tom and the other to be Mr. Hill. Then play the first part of the dialog. Pupils listen and repeat. Continue in the same way with the rest of the dialog.

AB 2 ex B **Match the sentences. Draw a line.**

- Pupils match the pictures and the sentences by drawing lines.

- Check by pointing at the pictures, and asking pupils to repeat what the characters are saying.

Key

1

Mr. Cooper:	Hello, Ben.
Ben:	Good morning, Mr. Cooper.

2

Tom and Jenny:	Bye, Miss Fisher.
Miss Fisher:	Goodbye, Tom and Jenny.

Ending the lesson

Game: Hello, Goodbye, Thank you

- Address each pupil by saying *Hello, (pupil's name)*; *Goodbye, (pupil's name)*; or by giving the pupil something, for example, a pencil. Pupils respond appropriately, either by saying *Hello, (teacher's name)*; *Goodbye, (teacher's name)*; or *Thank you*.

- Explain how to play the game in L1. After playing the game for some time, pupils continue without the teacher. Each pupil chooses another member of the class to respond.

Lesson 3

> **Language**
>
> Hello/Hi, I'm (Jill).

Beginning the lesson

- Practice greeting the pupils individually, with pupils responding: *Good morning, (pupil's name). Good morning, (teacher's name).*

 A chant

Listen and say.

- Play the chant on cassette. Pupils listen and follow in their books.

- Play the chant again, pausing for pupils to repeat. Then pupils listen and read aloud. Repeat until pupils can do the chant with books closed.

- Divide the class into two groups and repeat the chant. One group is Miss Fisher, the other Tom and Jenny.

- Pupils practice the chant in pairs, substituting their own names.

Draw and write.

- Each pupil draws their own picture and another of a friend in the picture frames. Underneath each picture they write *Hi, I'm ...* with their name and their friend's name.

- Go around the class helping pupils to write. Ask pupils to show each other their pictures and guess who they have drawn before reading the writing underneath.

Who is it? Listen and circle the right answer.

- Explain that Mr. Cooper is talking to someone in each picture but we can't see who it is. Pupils

must listen to find out who Mr. Cooper is talking to.

- Play the cassette. Pupils listen and circle the right answer.

Tapescript and key

1
Tom:	Good morning, Mr. Cooper.
Mr. Cooper:	Hello, Tom. (Tom)

2
Miss Fisher:	Good morning, Mr. Cooper.
Mr. Cooper:	Good morning, Miss Fisher. (Miss Fisher)

3
Jenny:	Hello, Mr. Cooper.
Mr. Cooper:	Hello, Jenny. (Jenny)

4
Ben:	Good morning, Mr. Cooper.
Mr. Cooper:	Good morning, Ben. (Ben)

- Check the answers with the whole class.

Ending the lesson

- Play the *Good morning* chant on the cassette and repeat the chant again with the class.

Lesson 4: Activity Lesson

> | **Language** | **New words and expressions** |
> |---|---|
> | Hello, I'm (Jenny). | make |
> | **Materials needed** | |
> | scissors, cloth, wool, glue, paper and poster paint | |

Beginning the lesson

- Play the game *Hello, Goodbye, Thank you.*

Make a puppet.

- If you have time, make a puppet before class to show pupils what they will be making. Otherwise look at the picture of the finished puppets. Ask pupils to decide what they want their puppets to represent: a boy, a girl or themselves.

- Go through the instructions step by step with the pupils.

- Pupils work in pairs or in groups, helping each other to make their puppets. Go around the class helping where necessary.

Using the puppets

- Pupils give their puppets names, which may be the names of some of the characters in the story.

- Pupils, in pairs, can make up dialogs for their puppets using the expressions they know, for example:

    A: Hi, I'm (Jenny).
    B: Hello, I'm (Mr. Cooper).
    A: Goodbye.
    B: Goodbye.

- Keep the puppets for use in future lessons.

Ending the lesson

 Say the *Good morning* chant again, using the puppets to represent the people in the chant.

Unit 2 How are you?

Background information

It is the end of the school day and Ben is leaving school. He says goodbye to his teacher and heads for Mr. Mendez's store. Because the store is near Ben's home and school, the storekeeper knows him and greets him by name.

Lesson 1

> **Language**
>
> Good afternoon
> *How are you today?
> *How are you this afternoon?
> *(I'm) fine, thanks.
> *he's/she's
> *Numbers 1 – 10

* = *new language*

Beginning the lesson

- Play the game from Unit 1: *Hello, Goodbye, Thank you.*

- Open Pupils' Books at page 6 and discuss the story in L1. Ask pupils what they think is happening, and explain anything they do not understand. Ask pupils to compare the store with a similar store in their own country.

- Introduce the numbers *1* to *10* using the numbers on the motif strip on page 6 of the Pupils' Book.

PB 6/7 How are you?

Listen and look.

 Listen to the cassette together while pupils follow the dialog in the Pupils' Book.

- Point to the pictures of Ben, Miss Fisher and Mr. Mendez and ask pupils to say their names.

- Explain the meaning of *How are you?* and *Fine, thanks.*

 Play the dialog again, pausing for pupils to repeat.

PB 8 ex 1 Find the people!

Listen and point.

- Ask pupils to say the names of the people in the picture.

- Play the cassette. Pupils listen and point to the correct picture.

Tapescript and key

Ben: I'm Ben. (1)
She's Miss Fisher. (3)
He's Mr. Hill. (5)
She's Jenny. (4)
He's Tom. (2)
He's Mr. Mendez. (6)

- Play the cassette again, pausing for pupils to repeat *She's Miss Fisher, He's Mr. Hill,* etc.

AB 5 ex A Write the words in the story.

- Explain that Little Red Riding Hood and Mr. Wolf are characters from a fairytale. Ask in L1 if the pupils have this story in their country. Can they remember the story?

- Read the words in the box aloud and explain that they are the missing words from the story.

- Pupils work on their own or in pairs finding the missing words and writing them in the blanks.

- Pupils can practice reading the dialog from the story in pairs.

Key
Mr. Wolf: Good afternoon, Little Red Riding Hood.
RRH: Good *afternoon*, Mr. Wolf.
Mr. Wolf: How are *you* today?

RRH: Fine, *thanks.*
RRH: *Goodbye,* Mr. Wolf.
Mr. Wolf: Goodbye.

Ending the lesson

Listen to the story on page 6 of the Pupils' Book again on the cassette.

- Pupils use their puppets to practice a dialog:

    A: How are you today?
    B: I'm fine, thanks.

- Review the numbers *1* to *10* by saying them in chorus.

Lesson 2

> **Language**
>
> How are you today?
> I'm fine, thanks.
> he's/she's

Beginning the lesson

- Review *How are you today?* and *I'm fine, thanks*:

    Teacher: How are you today?
    Pupils: I'm fine, thanks.

- Ask pairs of pupils to practice saying this dialog, with or without puppets.

- Ask pupils in L1 to tell you what is happening in the picture story on page 6 and 7 of the Pupils' Book. Ask them to find and point to the words *How are you?* and *Fine, thanks.*

PB 8 ex 2 **Who are they?**

Read and match.

- Ask pupils to identify the people in the pictures. Help them to make sentences: *She's Miss Fisher,* etc.

- Point to the sentences in the speech bubbles and read them aloud with the class.

- In pairs, pupils match the sentences to the people in the pictures.

Key

1 He's Mr. Mendez.
2 She's Miss Fisher.
3 He's Ben.
4 She's Jenny.
5 He's Mr. Hill.

- Point to the pictures in turn and ask pupils to say the sentences aloud.

 Give each pupil some paper and ask them to draw a picture of someone in the class. Hold up some examples and ask pupils to guess who they are: *He's ..., She's ...,* etc. Then ask them all to show their pictures to their partners so that they can guess who they have drawn.

AB 5 ex B **Write *he's* or *she's*.**

- Look at the pictures and ask pupils if they recognize the fairytale characters.

- Say some examples first, to make sure that all pupils understand that *she* refers to a female and *he* to a male.

Key

1 *He's* Mr. Wolf.
2 *She's* Little Red Riding Hood.
3 *She's* Cinderella.
4 *He's* Aladdin.
5 *She's* Snow White.
6 *He's* Pinocchio.

- Pupils finish the sentences beside each character. Check the answers with the whole class.

Ending the lesson

- Write the numbers *1* to *10* on pieces of paper or card. Give them to ten different pupils in the class. Ask the class to identify the pupils as you call out the numbers.

    Teacher: Three. (*Pupil holds up number.*)
    Pupils: He's Carlos.

Lesson 3

Language

How are you?
I'm fine, thanks.
he's/she's

Beginning the lesson

- Ask pupils to identify people in the class using *he's* and *she's*. An alternative would be to use magazine pictures of famous people for pupils to identify.

- Review the numbers *1* to *10*. Count on your fingers as pupils say the numbers out loud.

- Then use the pictures on pages 6 and 7 of the Pupils' Book to practice numbers and counting.

    Pupils: One, two, three, four, five, six, seven.

 Good morning

Song.

 Introduce the song following the procedure described on page 7.

- As pupils sing along, they can mime saying *good morning* to each other.

AB 6 ex C | Write a puppet play.

- Pupils can work in pairs or on their own. They write what the puppets are saying under the pictures. Do the first two sentences with the whole class to make sure that pupils know what to do.

- Check the answers with the whole class.

Key

1 Hello, I'm Miss Dee.
2 He's *Mr. Day.*
3 How *are* you, *today?*
4 Fine, *thanks.*
5 Goodbye, *Mr. Day.*
6 *Goodbye, Miss Dee.*

- Pupils can try this dialog with their own puppets that they made in Unit 1, Lesson 4, substituting the names for their puppets' names.

Ending the lesson

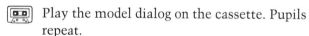 Sing the song *Good morning* again. Divide the class into two groups to sing alternate verses.

Lesson 4

Language

How are you today?
Numbers 1 – 10.

Beginning the lesson

- Sing the *Good morning* song with actions.

- Call out the numbers *1* to *10*. Ask pupils to show the right number of fingers for each number.

PB 9 ex 4 | What are they saying?

Talk to your friend.

- Pupils work in pairs, guessing what the characters in the pictures are saying. Explain what they have to do in L1.

Play the model dialog on the cassette. Pupils repeat.

- Go around the class helping children to make up what the characters are saying:

Key

Picture 2
Hello, Tom. How are you today?
Fine, thanks.

Picture 3
Hi, Jenny. How are you today?
Fine, thanks.

 Ask pupils to practice greeting each other in the same way. Each pupil writes his or her name on a piece of paper. Then mix the papers together. Pupils in turn draw a piece of paper and greet the pupil whose name is on it.

A: Hi, (Maria). How are you today?
B: I'm fine, thanks.

- If the class is very large, it may be better to divide the pupils into groups for this activity.

AB 7 ex D **Write the words in the puzzle.**

- Write the first word in the crossword puzzle with the whole class. Then pupils can continue on their own or with their partner.

Key

¹t	o	d	²a	y		³f			
			f			i			
			⁴t	h	a	n	k	s	
⁵g	o	o	d	b	y	e		e	
			r						
		⁶m	o	r	n	i	n	g	
			o						
⁷h	e	l	l	o					
			n						

AB 7 ex E **Listen. Write the numbers.**

Play the cassette. Pupils listen to the sounds and write the numbers.

Tapescript and key

1 (A car).
2 (A bird).
3 (A lion).
4 (A girl singing).
5 (A plane).
6 (A telephone).
7 (A frog diving into water).
8 (A dog).
9 (A boy beating a drum).
10 (A horse).

- Check the answers with the whole class.

- Play a game. Using the pictures and numbers in the Activity Book, call out a number and the pupils imitate the sound that goes with it.

Ending the lesson

- Ask pupils to count different things in the classroom in L1. (Make sure there are ten or fewer.)

    Teacher: (L1) Count the windows.
    Pupils: One, two, three, four.

Sing the song: *Good morning.*

Assessment activity

- To see if pupils can identify people using *he's* and *she's*.

- Cut out magazine pictures of well-known people (male and female) for pupils to identify. Pupils can write sentences: *He's Michael Jackson*, etc.

Unit 3 What's your name?

Background information

The scene of the story is in Ben's classroom, at the beginning of the day's lessons. This is a typical elementary school classroom in America. The principal of the school, Mr. Jones, appears and introduces a new pupil, Jill Brown, and her mother. The adults say "How do you do?" and shake hands when they meet. Children of Ben's and Jill's age do not usually say "How do you do?" or shake hands at their first meeting.

Lesson 1

Language	New words and expressions
Instructions:	
*Sit down.	children
*Stand up.	please
*Open your books.	How do you do?
*Close your books.	
*Quiet, please.	
*This is (Jill).	
*Mrs.	
*My name's (Ben).	

* = *new language*

Beginning the lesson

- Sing the song *Good morning*.

- Ask the class to say the numbers *1* to *10* out loud. Write the numbers at random on the blackboard and ask individual pupils to come to the front of the class and point to them: *Maria, point to six*. Pupils can also call out numbers for other pupils to find and point to.

PB 10/11 What's your name?

Listen and look.

- Open Pupils' Books at page 10 and discuss the story in L1. Ask pupils to find the characters they know in the pictures: Miss Fisher, Ben, Jenny, Tom. Encourage them to make sentences: *He's Ben, She's Miss Fisher*, etc.

- Ask them to compare the classroom in the picture with their own classroom. What is the same? What is different?

- Then ask them to say what they think is happening in the pictures (a new pupil is arriving).

- Listen to the cassette together. Pupils follow the text in the Pupils' Book.

- Ask pupils to point to the characters: Miss Fisher, Mr. Jones, Mrs. Brown, Jill, Ben. Explain in L1 that Jill's full name is Jill Brown, and her mother's name is Mrs. Brown.

- Play the cassette again, pausing for pupils to repeat.

- You could use the motif strip to teach useful classroom vocabulary: *book, pencil, pen, eraser, pencil case, ruler*.

PB 12 ex 1 What are they saying?

Look and say.

- Ask pupils to identify the characters in the pictures. Play the model dialog on the cassette and then ask pupils to read aloud the first example: *Hi. My name's Ben*. Practice saying *Hi, my name's ...* with the whole class.

- Ask pupils to practice the other examples in pairs. Go around the class helping pupils and hearing them speak.

- Ask pupils to practice introducing themselves in the same way. They can also use their puppets for extra practice.

AB 8 ex A Match the words and the pictures.

- Practice the instructions: *Sit down, please. Open your books, please*. Demonstrate and then ask pupils to follow your instructions: *Sit down, please*. (Pupils sit.) *Open your books, please*. (Pupils open their books). Explain the meaning of *Quiet, please*.

- From now on, use these English instructions in class, where appropriate.

- Introduce extra instructions: *Stand up* and *Close your books*. Practice with the class.

- Talk about the pictures in L1. Explain that Zap is a boy from the future and Rover is his dog. Ask pupils to tell you what is different about Rover (he's a robotic dog).

- Read the sentences in the exercise aloud. Pupils write the number of the correct picture next to the sentences. Check the answers with the whole class.

Key

My name's Zap. (1)
This is Rover. (5)
Sit down, Rover. (3)
Quiet please, Rover. (2)
Stand up, Rover. (4)

Ending the lesson

- Practice giving the instructions again: *Sit down, please. Stand up, please. Open your books, please. Close your books, please.* Pupils can give instructions, too.

Lesson 2

Language

Good morning, children.
This is Ben.
Hello/Hi, how are you?
I'm fine, thanks.
Instructions:
Stand up.
Sit down.
Open your book.
Close your book.

Beginning the lesson

- Greet the pupils in English: *Good morning/afternoon, children.* Ask them to respond: *Good morning/afternoon, Miss/Mrs./Mr. ....*

 **Stand up**

Listen and point.

- Ask pupils to identify the four children in the pictures: Jenny, Ben, Jill and Tom. They should say: *This is Jenny*, etc.

 Play the cassette. Pupils listen and point.

Tapescript

Stand up, Ben!
Sit down, Tom!
Open your book, Jenny!
Close your book, Jill!

- Ask pupils to read the instructions and match them with the pictures.

Pupils practice similar instructions in pairs, using their friends' names.

 What are they saying?

Listen and point.

- Talk about the pictures in L1. Ask pupils to guess what the people in the pictures are saying.

 Play the cassette. Pupils listen and point.

Tapescript

1
Hi, Simon.
Hi, Clare.

2
Hello, Mrs. Robinson. How are you?
I'm fine thanks, Mr. White.

3
Sit down, Spider.

AB 8 ex B **Write the story.**

- Talk about the story in L1. Ask pupils to describe what is happening. (Mr. Wolf meets Red Riding Hood's grandmother, Mrs. Little. Mr. Wolf acts in a friendly way, but his intentions are bad.)

- This exercise can be done orally with the whole class before pupils write, or pupils can work in pairs or groups to complete the conversation between Mr. Wolf and Mrs. Little.

Key

Mr. Wolf:	Hello, my *name's* Mr. Wolf.
Mrs. Little:	My *name's* Mrs. Little.
Mr. Wolf:	How *are you* today?
Mrs. Little:	Fine, thanks.
	Sit down, Mr. *Wolf.*

* Ask pupils to act out the conversation in pairs. They may use the finger puppets at the back of the book. Keep the finger puppets for future lessons.

Ending the lesson

Game: Mr. Wolf says ...

* Give instructions: *Mr. Wolf says stand up. Mr. Wolf says open your books*, etc. Pupils follow these instructions. Pupils must only do what they are told when they hear the words *Mr. Wolf says ...* . If you say just *Open your books* pupils must not do anything. Pupils who forget this rule are out of the game.

Lesson 3

Language	New words and expressions
My name's (Jill).	Be quiet!
This is (Ben).	
Instructions:	
(Stand up, etc.)	

Beginning the lesson

* Ask pupils to introduce themselves and each other to the class:

Pupil:	Hi. My name's Paul and this is Maria.
Class:	Hi, Paul and Maria.

* Use gestures to encourage pupils to say *stand up; sit down; quiet, please; open your books; close your books.*

 How do you do?

Song.

 Read the words of the song with the whole class. Play the cassette. Pupils listen.

Play the cassette again. Pupils listen and sing. The class can be divided into two groups for this song. The whole class sings the first two lines, the boys sing the third line, the girls sing the fourth and fifth lines, and the boys sing the last line.

* Pupils could also write a verse substituting their own names.

 Listen and number the pictures.

Pupils listen to the cassette and write the numbers next to the correct pictures. Pause the cassette after the first example, so that the whole class can do it together.

Tapescript

1 Good morning, children.
2 Sit down, please.
3 Open your books.
4 Close your books.
5 Stand up.
6 Be quiet.

Key

Reading across, the correct order of the pictures is: 1, 6, 2, 5, 3, 4.

* Check the answers with the whole class.

 Pupils now write what the teacher is saying in the pictures, using the words in the box. Play the cassette again while pupils listen. Write the first two examples with the whole class, then ask pupils to work in pairs or individually to write the words in the other pictures.

* Check the answers with the whole class.

Ending the lesson

* Play the game *Mr. Wolf says ...* .

* Sing the song *How do you do?* again.

Lesson 4: Activity Lesson ▩

> **New words and expressions**
>
> cut, draw, stick, paint
>
> **Materials needed**
>
> scissors, glue, poster paint, paper, colored pencils, large cardboard box or boxes

Beginning the lesson

- Play the game *Mr. Wolf says ...* .

 Make a puppet theater.

- You can divide pupils into groups for this activity. Or only make one theater for the whole class. Ask individual pupils to the front of the class to help you at each stage.

- Explain that pupils are going to make a puppet theater to use with their puppets.

- It may be necessary to cut the boxes for the pupils if the cardboard is thick. Tell pupils to design scenery to stick inside their theater (this could include changes of scenery, for example an indoor and an outdoor scene) and to decorate the outside with stick-on curtains, etc.

- As pupils work, introduce some of the classroom language for activity lessons: *cut, glue, draw*.

- Pupils can use their puppets to give a performance. This could be an enactment of the story on pages 10 and 11 of the Pupils' Book, or the dialog between Mr. Wolf and Mrs. Little in the Activity Book, page 8, exercise B.

- Pupils could go on to write their own plays, using the language learned so far, with different characters, taken for instance from a favorite television program.

- Keep the puppet theater or theaters for use in future lessons.

Ending the lesson

- Ask pupils to say the numbers *1* to *10*. They can say the numbers together and then take turns around the class.

Game: Bingo!

- Show pupils how to make cards. Draw a three-by-three square so there are nine spaces.

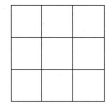

Write in numbers in random order. Call out the numbers. When pupils hear one of their numbers they should cross it out. The first pupil to complete a row of crosses shouts *Bingo!* and wins the game.

🖭 Sing the song *How do you do?* again.

Assessment activity

- Test individual pupil's ability to follow instructions by asking them to do things: *Stand up, sit down*, etc.

Unit 4 Ben's family

Background information

Jill meets Ben's family, the Taylors, after school. Ben introduces his mother and his elder brother and sister, Eddy and Mary, who are doing their homework, his father and his little sister, Sally, who are in the kitchen. The children's grandparents are visiting the family, drinking coffee and eating cookies, and they are introduced, too. Finally, Jill meets the family's pets, the dog, Mozart, and the cat, Elvis.

Lesson 1

Language	New words and expressions
*my/her/his	*Family:*
*What's your name?	Mom
*His name's ...	Dad
*Her name's ...	mother
	father
	sister
	brother
	grandfather
	grandmother
	dog
	cat
	friend
	house
	Come in.

Beginning the lesson

- Greet the class in English. Ask: *How are you today?* Pupils reply *Fine, thanks.* Play *Mr. Wolf says ...* with the language learned so far.

- Pupils practice introducing themselves. *Hi, my name's ....*

 **Ben's family**

Listen and look.

- Open Pupils' Books at page 14 and discuss the story in L1. Explain that Ben is taking Jill to meet his family. Point to the characters in the

motif strip and ask pupils to guess who the different members of the family are: Ben's mother, his sister, his brother, his father, his little sister and his grandparents.

- Ask pupils to compare Ben's family's house with their own homes.

 Listen to the cassette. Pupils follow the story in the Pupils' Book.

- Teach pupils the words *sister, brother, father, grandmother, grandfather, dog, cat.* Ask pupils to find and point to these words in the story on pages 14 and 15 of the Pupils' Book.

- Ask pupils to point to the people in the story: *Point to Ben's mother.* (Pupils point.) Do the same with Mary, Eddy, Ben's father, Sally, Ben's grandfather, Ben's grandmother, Mozart, Elvis.

- Explain that Ben calls his mother *Mom* and his father *Dad.*

 Play the dialog again, pausing for pupils to repeat.

PB 16 ex 1 This is my sister

Listen and point.

- Talk about the picture in exercise 1 in L1. Where are Ben's family? What are they doing? Tell pupils that they are going to hear Ben talking about his family on the cassette. They must point to the people as he describes them.

 Play the cassette. Pupils listen and point.

Tapescript and key

Ben: Look! This is Mary. She's my sister. (6)
And this is Eddy. He's my brother. (5)
This is Mozart. He's my dog. (8)
And this is my mother. (2)
And this is Elvis. He's my cat. (9)
And this is my father. (1)
This is Sally. She's my sister. (7)
This is my grandmother and this is my grandfather. (4 and 3)

Play the cassette again. This time pupils call out the numbers of the members of Ben's family as they are mentioned on the cassette.

Write *his* or *her*.

- Make sure that pupils understand that *his* refers to a male character and *her* to a female one. Refer them to Ben's family to practice: *This is Ben's brother. His name's Eddy. This is Ben's sister. Her name's Sally.* Then look at the first example in exercise A together.

- Pupils write *his* or *her* in the gaps. Check the answers with the whole class.

Key

1 *His* name's Robert.
2 *Her* name's Katie.
3 *Her* name's Sureena.
4 *His* name's Martin.
5 *His* name's John.
6 *Her* name's Sophie.

Ending the lesson

- Ask pupils to introduce their friends to the class. *This is my friend. Her name's Maria.*

Lesson 2

Language

What's your name?
Is this (Jenny)?
Yes./No.
he's/she's

Materials needed

paper for drawing

Beginning the lesson

- Greet pupils in English then practice the dialog.

    A: Hi, what's your name?
    B: My name's (Maria).

- Pupils practice around the class and in pairs.

 Is this Mrs. Taylor?

Talk to your friend.

 Teach the question and answer. *Is this ...? Yes. Is this ...? No, he's/she's ... .* Play the model dialog on the cassette. Pupils listen and repeat.

- Bring three or four pupils to the front of the class. Ask questions about them.

    Teacher: Is this (Maria)?
    Pupils: No, she's (Pilar).
    Teacher: Is this Maria?
    Pupils: Yes.

- Pupils work in pairs to talk about the pictures in exercise 2 on page 16 of the Pupils' Book. Check the answers with the whole class.

Key

Is this Mrs. Taylor?	Is this Mozart?
No, she's Miss Fisher.	No, he's Elvis.
Is this Jill?	Is this Mr. Taylor?
No, she's Mary.	No, he's Eddy.

Pupils draw pictures of people they know, then ask their friends questions about them.

    A: Is this Carlos?
    B: No, he's my brother.

Find nine words in the square.

- Pupils find the words in the square, following the example. When they have found the words, pupils write them down.

- Check the answers with the whole class.

Key

mother, brother, friend, house, cat, name, dog, sister, father

B	M	U	I	H	E	R
R	F	R	I	E	N	D
O	H	O	U	S	E	D
T	X	Y	C	A	T	O
H	N	A	M	E	Z	G
E	S	I	S	T	E	R
R	F	A	T	H	E	R

Ending the lesson

Game: Is this ...?

- Blindfold a pupil. Invite another pupil to the front of the class. Other pupils in the class ask *Is this ...?* The blindfolded pupil must say either *yes* or *no*.

- Ask pupils to bring photos of their own families for the next lesson.

Lesson 3

> **Language**
>
> **Possessive 's*:
> This is Jill's mother.

* = *new language*

Beginning the lesson

- Greet the pupils in English. Point to a pupil and ask *What's her/his name?* Pupils answer. Continue around the class.

- Use the pictures pupils drew in Lesson 2 to ask questions:

    A: Is this Maria?
    B: Yes.
    A: Is this Carlos?
    B: No, he's ... .

PB |17| ex 3 Yoko and Stefan

Read about Yoko's family.
Talk to your friend about Stefan's family.

- Discuss the photographs of Yoko and Stefan in L1. Ask pupils to guess how old the children are and where they come from. Ask pupils (L1) to look at the photos of their houses. How are they different to pupils' homes?

- Demonstrate the possessive 's. Use pictures from the Pupils' Book or Activity Book or draw a family on the board say: *This is Zap's dog. This is Red Riding Hood's grandmother*, etc.

- Pupils read about Yoko's family. Say: *Point to Yoko's mother*. Pupils point. Ask questions

about Yoko's family: *Is this Yoko's grandfather?* *(No, he's Yoko's father).*

- In pairs, pupils talk about Stefan's family.

    A: This is Stefan's mother.
    B: Is this Stefan's brother?
    A: Yes. *etc.*

 Pupils can talk about their own families in the same way. Go around the class, asking questions and helping pupils with their questions and answers.

AB |12| ex C Find Sophie's family.

Draw a line.

- Pupils look at the pictures and identify the members of Sophie's family by writing the number of the picture next to the correct sentence. Check the answers with the whole class.

    Key

    1 Sophie's brother.
    2 Sophie's mother.
    3 Sophie's grandfather.
    4 Sophie's sister.
    5 Sophie's grandmother.
    6 Sophie's father.

- Ask pupils to write about Sophie's family, following the example.

    Key

    1 Joe is Sophie's brother.
    2 Mrs. Grey is Sophie's mother.
    3 Mr. Allen is Sophie's grandfather.
    4 Hilary is Sophie's sister.
    5 Mrs. Allen is Sophie's grandmother.
    6 Mr. Grey is Sophie's father.

AB |13| ex D Draw and write about your family.

- Pupils draw pictures in the photo frames and write about members of their own families.

- Ask pupils to show their drawings to their friends and talk about them.

Ending the lesson

- Sing one of the songs from Units 1 to 3.

Lesson 4

Language	New words and expressions
Is this (Jenny)?	Grandpa
Yes./No.	Grandma
Materials	
puppets and puppet theater	

Beginning the lesson

- Play the game *Is this ...?*

 My family

Song.

- Introduce the song. Explain that *Grandpa* and *Grandma* are the names children call their grandparents (like *Mom* and *Dad* for *mother* and *father*).

- Divide the class into groups so that they can sing this song as a round.

Listen. Answer the questions yes or *no*.

- Tell pupils that this is Zap's family. Talk about the pictures in L1. Ask pupils what the characters in the pictures are doing and to try to guess who they are.

 Play the cassette. Pupils listen and draw a circle around the right answer, *yes* or *no*.

Tapescript

1 This is my father.
2 This is my sister.
3 This is my brother.
4 This is my cat.
5 This is my mother.
6 This is my grandfather.

- Check the answers with the whole class.

Key

1 yes **2** no **3** yes **4** yes **5** no **6** yes

- Pupils can talk about the pictures in pairs: *This is Zap's father*, etc.

Ending the lesson

- In groups, pupils make up a play, based on the story from this unit, to perform with their puppets, for example:

  A: This is my brother. His name's Zap.
  B: Hello, Zap.
  C: Hello. This is my dog. His name's Rover.
  D: Woof! Woof!

Assessment activity

- This activity is designed to see if pupils can write about their friends and families, using *this is*.

- Draw simple pictures on the board of a boy with his parents and a girl with her parents.

- Check pupils understand the difference between *his* and *her*. Say: *Show me his mother, show me her father*, etc. Pupils point.

- Pupils can copy the pictures and write about them, e.g.
  This is Susan. This is her mother. This is her father.
  This is Robert. This is his mother. This is his father.

Unit 5 What's this?

Background information

Mary Taylor is watching her little sister, Sally, drawing and is talking to her about it.

In the background Mozart and Elvis are fighting over Mozart's food.

Lesson 1

Language	New words and expressions
*Show me (a picture).	
*your	picture
*What's this?	dog
*Is it a (dog)?	cat
*It's a cat.	bird
	plane
	school
	car
	bus
	too
	I see.

* = *new language*

Beginning the lesson

- Greet the class in English. Ask questions to review language so far: *How are you today? What's your/her/his name? Is this ...?*

- Play the game *Mr. Wolf says ... .*

PB 18/19 What's this?

Listen and look.

- Open Pupils' Books at page 18 and ask pupils to tell you the names of the people and animals they can see in the pictures: Mary, Sally, Mozart and Elvis. Discuss the story in L1. Where are Mary and Sally? What are they doing? What are Mozart and Elvis doing?

- Teach the new words *bird, plane, school, car, bus* by referring to the motif strip.

- Listen to the cassette. Pupils follow the story in the Pupils' Book.

- Ask questions about Sally's pictures: *What's this? (It's a dog.) What's this? (It's a cat.),* etc.

- Play the dialog again, pausing for pupils to repeat.

- In pairs, pupils ask questions about Sally's pictures.

    A: What's this?
    B: It's a bus.

PB 20 ex 1 Jill's picture

Listen and point.

- Ask pupils to listen to Jill talking to her mother about her picture. Pupils point to the things in the picture as Jill mentions them. Pause the cassette to check that pupils are pointing to the right thing.

- Play the cassette. Pupils listen and point.

Tapescript and key

Jill:	Look, Mom. This is my picture!
Mrs. Brown:	Oh, it's very good.
Jill:	Look! This is a school. And this is a bus.
Mrs. Brown:	What's this?
Jill:	It's a cat – and this is a dog! And look! This is a house.
Mrs. Brown:	Is this a bird?
Jill:	No. It's a plane. *This* is a bird.
Mrs. Brown:	And this is my car!

- Pupils talk about the picture in pairs.

    A: What's this?
    B: It's a school. Is this a cat?
    A: Yes.

AB $^{14}_{ex\,A}$ **Write the sentences.**

- Ask questions about the pictures: *What's this? It's a ... .*

- Ask pupils to write the sentences, using the story in the Pupils' Book to help them with the spelling.

- Check the answers with the whole class.

  Key

  1 It's a plane.
  2 It's a car.
  3 It's a picture.
  4 It's a house.
  5 It's a bird.
  6 It's a bus.

Ending the lesson

Game

- Draw something in the air with your finger. Pupils must guess what your are drawing. The pupil who guesses correctly has the next turn.

  A: Is it a plane?
  B: No.
  A: Is it a bird?
  B: Yes.

Lesson 2

Language	New words and expressions
What's this?	rat
It's a (cat).	horse
Is it a (bird)?	Help!
*No, it's a (plane).	
Materials needed	
puppets and puppet theater	

* = *new language*

Beginning the lesson

- Play the drawing in the air game from Lesson 1.

PB $^{20}_{ex\,2}$ **What's this?**

Look at the pictures.

- Discuss the photographs in L1. Explain that they are pictures from around the world: a school in Kenya, a house in Thailand, a bus in Boston U.S.A., a flamingo and a dog from China.

- Play the model dialog on the cassette. Pupils listen and repeat.

- In pairs, pupils talk about the pictures.

- Ask questions about the pictures with the whole class: *What's this? (It's a dog.) Is this a house? (No, it's a school.)*, etc.

AB $^{14}_{ex\,B}$ **Complete the crossword.**

- Teach the two new words *rat* and *horse* that pupils need to complete the crossword.

- Pupils use the pictures to fill in the crossword puzzle, working on their own or in pairs.

  Key

  1 picture
  2 plane
  3 bird
  4 school
  5 rat
  6 bus
  7 horse
  8 house

AB $^{15}_{ex\,C}$ **Write the story.**

- Look at the pictures with the class and discuss the story in L1: What is Mr. Wolf planning? Why is he wearing Mrs. Little's clothes? Then ask pupils in pairs to write the words in the story.

- Check the answers with the whole class.

  Key

  Girl: Sh! Quiet!
  Boy: Is it Mrs. Little?
  Girl: *No.*
  Boy: *Is it* a dog?
  Girl: *No.*
  Boy: Help!
  Girl: It's a *wolf/Mr. Wolf!*

- Ask pupils to practice the dialog in pairs.

Ending the lesson

- Pupils act out the story from exercise C in the Activity Book with puppets and the puppet theater.

Lesson 3

Language	New words and expressions
*It isn't ...	ship
	train
	hen
	rat
	Listen!
Materials needed	
magazine pictures	

* = new language

Beginning the lesson

- Show the pupils a magazine picture of something they know the English word for, e.g. a car or a house. Hide it from the pupils, and ask them to guess what it is.

Pupil:	Is it a dog?
Teacher:	No.
Pupil:	Is it a school?
Teacher:	No.

 **Listen!**

Song.

Introduce and practice the song in the usual way.

Divide the class into groups. Pupils sing alternate verses. They can also try to imitate the sound effects.

 **What is it?**

Listen to the sounds and point to the pictures.

Tell pupils that they are going to hear some sounds. Play the cassette. Pupils listen and point.

Tapescript and key

1 (Dog).

2 (Cat).
3 (Plane).
4 (Bird).
5 (Hen).

Play the cassette again. Pause after each sound and ask a question: *What is it? (It's a dog.)*, etc.

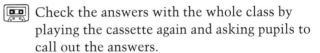 **Listen. Answer yes or no.**

Play the cassette. Pupils look at the pictures, listen and draw a circle around the right answer *yes* or *no*.

Tapescript and key

1 What is it? Is it a bus? (yes)
2 What's this? Is it a plane? (no)
3 What's this? Is it a school? (no)
4 Is this Mrs. Little? (no)
5 Is this Red Riding Hood? (yes)
6 Is this Mr. Wolf's house? (yes)

Check the answers with the whole class by playing the cassette again and asking pupils to call out the answers.

Ending the lesson

Sing the song *Listen!* again.

Lesson 4: Activity Lesson

New words and expressions
Very good.
Materials needed
scissors, paper, colored pens, glue, cardboard and string to make a folder
Two sets of six cards or pieces of paper with the words *dog, cat, plane, car, hen, bird* written on them.

Beginning the lesson

- Divide class into two teams and give each team a set of six cards with the words dog, cat, etc. A pupil from each team takes a card, makes the appropriate noise and asks his or her team *What's this?* The first team to guess wins a point and the team with the most points wins the game.

 PB 21 ex 5 | **Is it a book?**

Game.

Play the model dialog on cassette. Pupils repeat. Teach the new expression *Very good*.

• Show pupils how to play the game. One pupil draws a picture, very slowly, line by line. His or her partner has to try and guess what it is before the picture is finished.

• In pairs, pupils play the game as shown in the Pupils' Book.

• Use pupils' pictures to ask the class questions: *What's this?* (*It's a house.*), etc.

AB 16 ex E | **Make a picture dictionary.**

• Pupils can make dictionaries in pairs, in which case the title would be *Our picture dictionary*.

• Pupils follow the instructions to make their picture dictionaries. Go around the class helping pupils and asking questions about the pictures in their dictionaries.

• These picture dictionaries should be kept. As pupils learn new words they can be written and illustrated in the dictionaries. They can use cut-out magazine pictures instead of drawings if they wish.

Ending the lesson

 Sing the song *Listen!* again with pupils making the sound effects.

Assessment activity

• Ask pupils to draw pictures of single objects, using English vocabulary they know, e.g. a car, a house.

• Pupils use these pictures to ask and answer questions. They should be able to ask *What's this?* and answer *It's a ... .*

Unit 6 Is this your hat?

Background information

It is a windy day in the fall and Mary, Ben and Jenny are going for a walk in the country near their home. They find a hat blowing along the country road. It turns out that the hat belongs to Fred, Mr. Reed's horse.

Lesson 1

Language	New words and expressions
What's this?	hat
It's a (hat).	jacket
*It isn't (my hat).	T-shirt
It's (Jenny)'s (hat).	skirt
my/your	sweater
*Whose (hat) is it?	dress
*Is it (Mary)'s (hat)?	scarf
Is this your (hat)?	coat
	I don't know.
	That's right.

* = *new language*

Beginning the lesson

- Greet the class in English. Ask questions: *How are you today? What's your name? What's this?* (pointing to pictures).

 Sing the song *Listen!* from Unit 5.

PB 22/23 Is this your hat?

Listen and look.

- Discuss the story on page 22 of the Pupils' Book in L1. Ask pupils to work out what is happening: it is a windy day, the children find a hat, they talk about the hat, they find out that the hat belongs to a horse.

- Use the motif strip and the pictures in the story to show pupils the kind of things you would see in the countryside. Ask (L1) if this is the same as in their country.

- Teach the key word *hat*.

 Listen to the cassette. Pupils follow the story in the Pupils' Book.

- Ask questions about the story in English.

    Teacher: What's this? *(Point to the hat.)*
    Pupil: It's a hat.
    Teacher: Is it Ben's hat?
    Pupil: No.
    Teacher: Is it Mary's hat?
    Pupil: No.
    Teacher: Is it Mr. Reed's hat?
    Pupil: No.
    Teacher: Whose hat is it?
    Pupil: It's Fred's hat.

 Play the dialog again, pausing for pupils to repeat.

PB 24 ex 1 Find the clothes!

Talk to your friend.

- Teach the words for clothes in the picture: *hat, jacket, T-shirt, skirt, sweater, dress, scarf, coat.* Say the words aloud. Pupils repeat.

- Play the model dialog on cassette. Practice the dialog with the whole class. Point to the pictures in the book and ask: *What's this? Whose hat is it?*

- Pupils work in pairs to find the clothes in the story on pages 22 and 23 of the Pupils' Book. Ask them in pairs to talk about the clothes, following the example in the Pupils' Book.

Key

Fred's hat; Ben's jacket; Jenny's sweater; Mary's dress; Jenny's skirt; Ben's T-shirt; Mary's scarf; Mary's coat.

AB 17 ex A Whose hat is this? Write sentences.

- In pairs, or on their own, pupils match the hats with their owners and write sentences.

- Check the answers with the whole class.

Key

1 It's Tom's hat.
2 It's Joe's hat.
3 It's Fred's hat.
4 It's Barbara's hat.
5 It's Caroline's hat.

- Pupils can talk about the hats in pairs.

Ending the lesson

- Pupils can add clothes vocabulary to their picture dictionaries: *hat, jacket, T-shirt, skirt, sweater, dress, scarf and coat.*

Lesson 2

Language	New words and expressions
these	glove
Whose are they?	shoe
This isn't (Ben)'s (jacket).	Pick it up.
	Look at …
Materials needed	
paper for drawing	

Beginning the lesson

- Ask questions about clothes. You can ask about the clothes pupils are wearing in class, or the ones in exercise 1 on page 24 of the Pupils' Book.

 PB 24 ex 1 **Draw a picture of your clothes.**

Pupils draw and label their own clothes, then talk to their friends about them.

    A: What's this?
    B: This is my (sweater).

- Pupils could also draw clothes belonging to other pupils in the class and then talk about them.

    A: Is this (Maria's sweater)?
    B: Yes.

- Save the drawings for further work later.

 PB 24 ex 2 **What are they saying?**

Listen and point.

Before listening to the cassette, identify the clothes in the pictures: *jackets, scarf, T-shirt, sweater.* Discuss what is happening in the pictures in L1. (The teacher is talking to the pupils about their jackets; the woman has found the man's scarf; the boys are getting ready for games; the father is angry with the girl, he wants her to pick up her sweater.)

- Teach *pick up.* Demonstrate with something in the classroom. *Pick up the book, Carlos.*

Play the cassette. Pupils listen and point.

Tapescript and key

1
Man: Caroline! Is this your sweater? Pick it up, please.
Caroline: OK.

2
Woman: Oh dear! Look at these jackets! Whose are they? Is this your jacket, Richard?
Richard: I don't know.

3
Boy: Is this your T-shirt, Steve?
Steve: No.
Boy: Whose T-shirt is it?
Steve: I don't know.

4
Rachel: Mr. Smith! Is this your scarf?
Mr. Smith: Oh thank you, Rachel!

Play the cassette again. Pause the cassette so that pupils can listen and repeat.

- Pupils can act out the dialogs, using their own names.

 AB 17 ex B **Write about Mr. Wolf.**

- Use pupils' own drawings for practice with *isn't.* Hold up a drawing and ask questions about it: *Is this (Maria's) jacket? (No, it isn't Maria's jacket.),* etc.

- Teach the new words *glove* and *shoe.* Ask pupils to point to and identify the clothes in the picture of Mr. Wolf on page 17 of the Activity Book:

Is this Mr. Wolf's shoe? (No.) *Whose shoe is this?*
(*It's Mrs. Little's shoe.*), etc.

- Pupils write sentences, following the example, working either alone or in pairs.

Key

1 This isn't Mr. Wolf's hat.
2 This isn't Mr. Wolf's scarf.
3 This isn't Mr. Wolf's jacket.
4 This isn't Mr. Wolf's glove.
5 This isn't Mr. Wolf's skirt.
6 This isn't Mr. Wolf's shoe.

- Ask questions about the picture: *Is this Mr. Wolf's hat? No, it isn't his hat.*

Ending the lesson

- Ask questions about pupils' drawings of their own clothes: *Whose sweater is this? It's Maria's sweater. Carlos, is this your T-shirt?*

Lesson 3

Language	New words and expressions
Put on (your sweater).	socks
Take off (your shoes).	Let's all go out to play.
*Plurals	It's time to go to bed.

* = *new language*

Beginning the lesson

- Play *Mr. Wolf says ... .* Include *Pick up your ...* in the instructions.

PB 25 ex 3 **Action rhyme**

Listen, say and do.

- Teach the new words for the action rhyme: *put on, take off, socks.* Explain the plural formed by adding *s.* Explain the meaning of *Let's all go out to play* and *It's time to go to bed.*

 Play the cassette. Pupils listen and repeat. Read the rhyme and mime the actions: putting on sweaters and jackets, gloves and hats, socks and shoes; taking off shoes and socks, gloves and hats, sweaters and jackets.

- Divide the class into two groups. One group repeats the rhyme, telling the other group what to do.

AB 18 ex C **Finish the questions. Write the answers.**

- In pairs or on their own, pupils write the questions and answers.

- Check the questions and answers orally with the whole class.

Key

1 Whose jacket is this? It's Hannah's.
2 Whose hat is this? It's Joe's.
3 Whose shoe is this? It's Sophie's.
4 Whose scarf is this? It's Kate's.
5 Whose glove is this? It's Mark's.

AB 18 ex D **Listen and circle the right answer.**

- Ask questions about the pictures: *What's this? (It's a jacket.)* Say: *Point to a plane.*

 Play the cassette. Pupils listen and draw a circle around the right answer.

Tapescript

1
Is this your hat, Martin?
No. It's Sophie's hat.

2
Is this your T-shirt, Sophie?
No. It's Martin's T-shirt.

3
Whose car is this?
It's Martin's.

4
Whose plane is this?
It's Sophie's.

5
Is this your book, Sophie?
Yes, it is.

6
Is this Martin's cat, Sophie?
Yes, it is.

- Check the answers.

  1 Sophie's
  2 Martin's
  3 Martin's
  4 Sophie's
  5 Sophie's
  6 Martin's

Ending the lesson

- Do the action rhyme again.

Lesson 4

Language

Put on (your jacket).
Take off (your shoes).
It's a (scarf).
Whose (scarf) is it?
It's (Jenny)'s.

Materials needed

a large box

Beginning the lesson

- Play *Mr. Wolf says ....* Mime the instructions as they are said: *(Carlos), take off your ... .*

 Is it a sweater?

Game.

- Explain the game as in exercise 4 on page 25 of the Pupils' Book. Ask each pupil in the class to give one item of clothing and put them all in a large box. A pupil puts on a blindfold and takes from the box an item of clothing, for example a sweater. He or she must guess whose it is.

 Play the model dialog on cassette. Pupils repeat, then play the game.

AB 19 ex E Write the story.

- Discuss the story in L1. Instead of the usual version of the story, this time Red Riding Hood spots the Wolf dressed up in her grandmother's clothes right away, and tells him to take them off.

- Pupils complete the story on their own or in pairs. Check the answers with the whole class.

Key

Mr. Wolf: Come in, Red Riding Hood.
RRH: This isn't my grandmother.
Take off my grandmother's *hat*.
Take off my grandmother's *gloves*.
Take off *my grandmother's shoes.*
Take off my grandmother's scarf.
Goodbye, Mr. Wolf.
Goodbye.

Ending the lesson

- Pupils act out the story of Red Riding Hood and Mr. Wolf in pairs. They could use the finger puppets from the back of the Activity Book.

Assessment activity

- To see if pupils can talk about possessions, using *Whose?*

- Hold up items of clothing or objects borrowed from pupils in the class. Tell pupils to ask and answer questions about them, e.g. *Whose bag is this? It's Ana's.*

Project ideas

Pupils can find out about traditional clothes worn in other countries and draw and label them.

Or they can design their own new fashion collection for the different seasons – spring, summer, winter and fall.

Unit 7 Happy birthday, Jill!

Background information

It is Jill's birthday, and she is having a birthday party. She is nine years old. Birthdays are celebrated in America by sending cards and giving birthday presents. Children often have parties for their birthdays, with birthday cakes. Children's birthday parties are usually held in the afternoon.

There is a birthday cake with nine candles and the children sing Happy Birthday to You. Jill will blow out the candles and make a wish. The children wear their best clothes and are given paper hats to wear at the party. The children will also play games.

Jill's friends each bring her a small present. Her grandfather has brought her a more expensive present, a watch.

Lesson 1

Language	New words and expressions
How old are you?	present
I'm (nine).	watch
Here's ...	purse
How old is (Tom)?	Happy birthday!
he's/she's (eight).	Thank you very much.

Beginning the lesson

- Repeat the action rhyme from Unit 6.

- Practice the numbers *1* to *10*. Pupils count aloud things in the classroom.

PB 26/27 Happy birthday, Jill!

Listen and look.

- Open Pupils' Books at page 26 and discuss the story in L1. Use the motif strip to ask pupils to guess what this unit is about (birthdays). Ask pupils to guess what is happening (It's Jill's birthday).

- If pupils celebrate birthdays in their country, they can compare birthday celebrations in America with those in their own country.

- Teach the key words *birthday* and *present*.

- Listen to the cassette. Pupils follow the story in the Pupils' Book.

- Teach the new word *watch* and the expression *Happy birthday*. Talk about the story in English: *Point to Jill, Point to Jill's grandfather; Show me the watch; Show me the purse.*

- Teach the question and answer: *How old are you? I'm ...* and practice the pupils' ages.

- Play the dialog again, pausing for pupils to repeat. Pupils sing *Happy birthday.*

PB 28 ex 1 How old is Dan?

Count the candles.

- Teach *birthday cake*. Ask questions about the birthday cakes. *Whose birthday cake is this? It's Dan's*, etc.

- Teach the question and answer: *How old is ...? She's/he's ... .* Ask *How old is Dan?* (Pupils count the candles). *He's eight.* Play the model dialog on cassette.

- In pairs, pupils talk about the other birthday cakes.

Key

A: How old is Dan?
B: He's eight.
A: How old is Sarah?
B: She's ten.
A: How old is Alice?
B: She's seven.
A: How old is Yasmin?
B: She's six.
A: How old is Peter?
B: He's nine.
A: How old is Steven?
B: He's five.

- Practice the questions and answers with the whole class.

AB 20 ex A Find the numbers in the square.

- Teach the spellings of the numbers *1* to *10*.

- Pupils find the numbers in the square. They can work on their own or in pairs.

- Check the answers with the whole class.

Key

```
S E V E N Q E
O N E S I X I
T F F I V E G
W O L M Z N H
O U T E N I T
Y R G B H N Q
T H R E E E Z
```

Ending the lesson

Sing *Happy Birthday to You* using the names of pupils in the class.

Lesson 2

Language

How old are you?
I'm (ten).
(Ben) is (nine) years old.

Materials needed

wrapped "present" for game

Beginning the lesson

- Ask pupils how old they are. *How old are you, (Carlos)? I'm (nine). How old is (Maria)? She's (eight).*

PB 28 ex 2 How old are you?

Who's talking? Listen and point.

- Discuss *birthday cakes* with pupils and remind them that they can tell how old someone is by counting the candles on the cake.

- Explain to pupils that these are photos of some of the children who have the birthday cakes in exercise 1. Point to the pictures and ask: *What's his name? He's Dan*, etc.

Play the cassette. Pupils listen and point to the person in the picture who is speaking.

Tapescript and key

Hello. How old are you today?
I'm eight.
Happy birthday!
Thanks.
(Dan)

Happy birthday! How old are you today?
I'm ten.
(Sarah)

Hello. What's your name?
Peter.
And how old are you?
I'm nine. It's my birthday today.
Happy birthday.
(Peter)

Hello. How old are you?
I'm six.
Happy birthday.
(Yasmin)

Play the model dialog on cassette. In pairs, pupils ask and answer questions, following the model dialog in the Pupils' Book.

AB 20 ex B How old are they? Follow the lines.

- Ask questions about the characters in the pictures: *Who's this? (It's Zap)*, etc. Pupils follow the lines to find the ages of the characters in the pictures, then write sentences about them.

Key

1 Zap is ten years old.
2 Rover is five years old.
3 Felina is four years old.
4 Arca is eight years old.
5 Delta is seven years old.

- Ask questions: *How old is Zap? He's ten years old.*

Ending the lesson

Game: Birthday present game.

- Give pupils a wrapped "present" to pass around the class. Pupils sing *Happy Birthday to You* while passing the "present" from one to another. When they get to the line *Happy birthday dear ...*, they put in the name of the pupil holding the present and then say: *Happy birthday (Maria). Here's your present.* He or she responds by saying *Thank you very much* and the game continues (without unwrapping the present).

Lesson 3

Language	New words and expressions
from	Here's your present.
What is it?	
It's a (watch).	

Beginning the lesson

- Play the *birthday present game.*

 What is it?

Follow the lines.

- Pupils look at the pictures of the wrapped presents first and try to guess what they are: *Is it a book? Is it a car?* etc. They then follow the lines and find out what the presents are.

- Check the answers by pointing to the parcels and asking: *What's this? (It's a book from Ben.).*

  Key

  The book is from Ben. The dog is from Mom and Dad. The pen is from Jenny. The scarf is from Polly. The car is from Joe. The cat is from Katie.

 Play the model dialog on the cassette. Pupils listen and repeat. In pairs, pupils role play Jill and the people giving her the birthday presents.

  Ben: Here's your present, Jill.
  Jill: What is it?
  Ben: It's a watch.
  Jill: Thank you very much.

 Find Red Riding Hood's five presents in the wood. Write sentences.

- Pupils on their own or in pairs find Red Riding Hood's five presents in the picture, then write sentences.

- Check the answers with the whole class.

  Key

  It's a purse.
  It's a car.
  It's a book.
  It's a watch.
  It's a scarf.

 Listen and write the ages on the cakes.

 Play the cassette. Pupils listen and write the ages on the cakes. Pause the cassette to give pupils time to write.

  Tapescript and key

  How old is John?
  He's eight years old.

  How old is Sophie?
  She's nine years old.

  How old is Martin?
  He's seven years old.

  How old is Kate?
  She's five years old.

- Check the answers with the whole class. Pupils draw the candles on the cakes. Pupils can practice the questions and answers in pairs.

Ending the lesson

 What is it?

Draw a birthday card.

 Pupils draw a birthday card, either to Jill or to one of their own friends.

Lesson 4: Activity Lesson

> **New words and expressions**
>
> fold
>
> **Materials needed**
>
> cardboard, colored paper, scissors, glue, poster paint, a pencil

Beginning the lesson

- Play the birthday present game.

AB 22 ex E **Make a birthday card.**

- Pupils follow the instructions in the Activity Book to make a pop-up birthday card. Make an example before the lesson, to show pupils what they will be making.

- If pupils know someone with a birthday soon, they can write *to ... from ...* in the card.

- Variations on the pop-up theme could be:

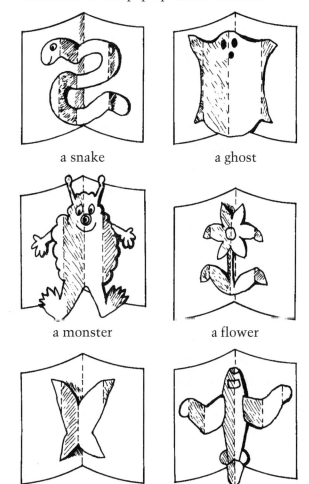

a snake	a ghost
a monster	a flower
a butterfly	a plane

Ending the lesson

- Pupils act out a birthday party, using the puppets and the puppet theater. They can make "props" out of cardboard, for example a present or presents and a birthday cake.

Assessment activity

- Ask pupils to draw a picture of a friend and write about him/her, e.g. *This is my friend. His name's Carlos. He's nine years old.*

- Pupils can also ask about each other's drawings, e.g. *What's her name? How old is she?*

Unit 8 Colors!

Background information

It is Saturday morning. The children, Ben, Tom, Jenny and Jill, are out playing a game in the street, in which they find and point to things with different colors. There is a farmer's market. Among the market stalls is a fruit and vegetable stall. Ben gets into trouble with the stallholder for knocking over some fruit and vegetables as he reaches out to show the others a cucumber.

Lesson I

Language	New words and expressions
*Tell me the name of something (blue).	blue
*are	yellow
*is/are + color	red
What's this?	orange
It's a (plane).	green
*What color is it?	brown
*It's (red).	black
	white
	pink
	purple
	the sky
	pants
	face
	bananas
	lemons
	truck
	apples
	oranges
	cucumbers
	Oh dear!

* = new language

Beginning the lesson

- Greet pupils in English and ask them questions about themselves: *How are you today? (I'm fine.) What's your name? How old are you?*

- Review the words for clothes: *hat, jacket, scarf, T-shirt, sweater, skirt, shoes, gloves, dress.* You could do this by asking questions about pictures in the Pupils' Book: *What's this? It's a hat. Whose hat is it? It's Fred's hat.* Then talk about pupils' own clothes. *Point to your shoes, Carlos*, etc.

- Pupils could play a version of *Mr. Wolf says ... : Mr. Wolf says point to your shoes*, etc.

PB 30/31 Colors!

Listen and look.

- Open Pupils' Books at page 30 and discuss the story in L1 and in English where possible: *(pointing) What's his name? Ben.* Ask pupils to tell you what they think the children are doing. Are they going to school? Why is the man angry with Ben in picture 5?

- Teach the key words: *blue, green, red, yellow, orange,* by referring the paint splashes on the motif strip.

- Listen to the cassette. Pupils follow the story in the Pupils' Book.

- Teach the new words: *pants, sky, face,* and the fruit and vegetables *bananas, lemons, oranges, apples, cucumbers.* Ask pupils to find and point to them in the pictures.

- Listen to the cassette again.

- Explain that *is* is used for singular words and *are* for plurals. Ask pupils to make sentences, as in the story: *Tell me the name of something blue. The sky is blue. Tell me the name of something yellow. Bananas are yellow.*

- Play the dialog again, pausing for pupils to repeat.

PB 32 ex 1 What color is it?

Listen and point.

- Look at exercise 1 and teach the additional colors *brown, black, white, pink, purple* by referring to the pictures. Pupils follow the lines to match the colors and the pictures.

39

Play the cassette. Pupils listen and point to the objects as Ben and Jill name them.

Tapescript and key

Ben: Show me something green.
Jill: This car's green.
Ben: Show me something red.
Jill: Mm ... The truck is red.
Ben: Now, show me something black.
Jill: The cat's black.
Ben: And ... er ... show me something purple.
Jill: Purple. The watch is purple. Now it's your turn. Show me something pink.
Ben: The jacket's pink.
Jill: Right. Show me something brown.
Ben: The dog's brown.
Jill: Show me something white.
Ben: The plane's white.
Jill: Show me something orange.
Ben: The sweater's orange.
Jill: Show me something blue.
Ben: The house is blue.
Jill: Yes ... Er ... Show me something yellow.
Ben: The bird's yellow.
Jill: Yes! Good!

 Play the model dialog on cassette: *What's this? It's a ... . What color is it? It's ... .* Pupils practice the dialog in pairs.

Ending the lesson

• Practice talking about colors with things in the class. Say: *Point to something green.* (Pupil points.)

Lesson 2

Language	New words and expressions
Tell me the name of something (blue). (The sky) is (blue).	witch favorite gray

Materials needed
pencils or crayons for coloring exercise in the Activity Book

Beginning the lesson

• Practice colors by pointing to things around the classroom: *What color is this? (It's red).*

• Review the names of fruit and vegetables using the pictures on page 31 of the Pupils' Book. *What are these? (Oranges.)*

PB 32 ex 2 Tell me the name of something green

Game.

 Play the model dialog on cassette. Pupils repeat.

• Practice the game with the whole class, then pupils continue in pairs. They can use the pictures in the Pupils' Book as well as things around the classroom. Give them some further vocabulary if they need it.

AB 23 ex A Color the picture.

• Pupils need the colors green, blue, brown, pink, black, red, gray and yellow to color the pictures. Teach the word *gray*.

• Pupils color the numbered parts of the picture and then write five sentences about it: *The sky is blue,* etc.

• Check the pupils' sentences. Ask questions about the pictures. *What color is the sky? It's blue,* etc.

AB 24 ex B Write the story.

• Discuss the story with the class in L1: Who are these people? Teach the new words *witch* and *favorite*. What is happening in the story?

• Pupils, on their own or in pairs, write the dialog for the story. Check the answers with the whole class.

Key

Willow: Hello. My *name's* Willow the witch. This *is* my *cat*.
Mr. Wolf: *Is* this your *house?*
Willow: Yes. My *favorite* color is black. What's your *favorite color?*
Mr. Wolf: Red.

- Pupils can practice the dialog between Willow and Mr. Wolf in pairs.

Ending the lesson

Game: What is it?

- Think of something that pupils can name in English. Say: *It's yellow. What is it?* Pupils must guess what it is: *Is it (a lemon)? No. Is it (Maria's dress)? Yes.*

Lesson 3

Language	New words and expressions
*What's your favorite color? *My favorite color is (red).	rainbow sun sea tree jeans *In song:* eyes summer skies true
Materials needed	
pencils or crayons for coloring Activity Book	

* = *new language*

Beginning the lesson

- Play the guessing game *Tell me the name of something green.*

 Can you color a rainbow?

Song.

- Teach the key vocabulary from the song: *rainbow, sun, sea, tree, eyes, summer, true, skies.*

 The song can be performed with actions. For example, pupils pretend to paint a rainbow in time with the music.

 What's your favorite color?

Talk to your friend.

🔲 Play the model dialog on cassette.

- Pupils ask their friends about their favorite colors. They can make a chart like this:

Name	Favorite color
Carlos	red
Maria	blue

- Alternatively, they can make a poster for the wall. Cut out shapes, for example, flowers, cars, stars. Pupils write their names on the cut-out shapes and color them in their favorite colors.

AB 24 ex C **Listen and color.**

- Pupils need blue, red, yellow, green and brown colored pens or pencils for this exercise.

🔲 Play the cassette. Explain that pupils must listen and color the clothes.

- Teach the new vocabulary: *jeans* (as worn by Maria).

- Pause after each section. Pupils listen and color.

Tapescript and key

Hello. My name's Maria. I'm ten years old. I'm wearing blue jeans and a red T-shirt.

This is my brother. His name's David. He's twelve. In this picture he's wearing a brown jacket and green pants.

And this is my friend Karen. She's ten years old. She's wearing her favorite dress. It's red and yellow.

- Check the answers by asking questions: *What color are Maria's jeans? (Blue.).*

Ending the lesson

- Ask pupils to draw their favorite clothes and color them. They can tell their partners about their pictures.

Lesson 4: Activity Lesson

> **Materials needed**
> scissors, cardboard, glue, colored pens, string

Beginning the lesson

- Talk about pupils' favorite colors: *Whose favorite color is blue?* Pupils raise hands. *What's your favorite color?*

 Make color spinners.

- The spinners will show pupils how two colors can combine to make a third color.

- Pupils follow the instructions on page 25 of the Activity Book. Make a color spinner before the lesson for pupils to look at.

- Pupils cut out a circle of cardboard about two or three inches in diameter. Pupils can draw the circles by drawing round a round shape such as a yogurt container. Help pupils to make the holes in their spinners. The string should be about twelve inches long.

- Ask pupils to spin their spinners to find out what colors appear. (Red and yellow make orange; red and blue make purple; and blue and yellow make green.)

Ending the lesson

- Pupils write the names of colors in their picture dictionaries.

- Sing the song *Can you color a rainbow?*

- Play the game *Tell me the name of something green.*

Assessment activity

- Bring objects of different colors to class. Hold them up and tell pupils to ask and answer: *What color is it? It's red.*

Project idea

- In groups, pupils collect magazine pictures of different colored things: one group collects pictures of blue things, another group collects pictures of yellow things, etc. This could be extended to include a display of small objects in the groups' colors.

Unit 9 Our street

Background information

Jenny is showing Jill the street where she lives. It is a fairly typical street in America. Each of the houses has a small back yard. The pictures show many of the things that you see on the street: telephone booth, mailbox, bus stop. The pictures also show some typical American leisure activities: painting the house, washing the car.

Lesson 1

Language	New words and expressions
Is this your (street)?	street
*This is (10) Lime Avenue.	number
*Who lives here?	Look!
*(Jenny) lives here.	telephone booth
*Who lives at (10 Lime Avenue)?	bus stop
*There's (Tom).	mailbox
	lives

* = *new language*

Beginning the lesson

- Play the game *Tell me the name of something green* (Unit 8).

 **Our street**

Listen and look.

- Open Pupils' Books at page 34 and discuss the story in L1. Ask pupils to tell you what they think the people in the pictures are doing.

- Ask pupils to compare the street where Jenny lives to their own home surroundings. Use the motif strip and the pictures in the story. Ask them to find the *telephone booth, bus stop and mailbox*.

- Teach the key words *street, lives*.

 Listen to the cassette. Pupils follow the story in the Pupils' Book.

- Ask questions about the story: *Who lives at 1 Lime Avenue? (Miss Fisher.) Who lives at 3 Lime Avenue? (Mr. Green.) Who lives at 9 Lime Avenue? (Tom.)* Say: *Point to Miss Fisher/Miss Fisher's house, Mr. Green/Mr. Green's car, Tom/Tom's tree.* (Pupils point.)

 Play the dialog again, pausing for pupils to repeat.

 Who lives at 2 Lime Avenue?

Listen and point.

- Explain the system of numbering houses in some parts of America where the odd numbered houses are on one side of the street and the even numbered houses are on the other. Is it the same in the country where the pupils live?

- This is the street in the story. Tell pupils that the name of the street is Lime Avenue. Ask pupils about the answers they already know from the story: *Who lives at 1 Lime Avenue? (Miss Fisher.) Who lives at 3 Lime Avenue? (Mr. Green.) Who lives at 9 Lime Avenue? (Tom.).*

 Play the cassette. Pupils listen and point to the houses.

Tapescript and key

Man:	This is Lime Avenue.
Woman:	Oh, yes. I see. Who lives at 1 Lime Avenue?
Man:	Miss Fisher. And Mr. Green lives at 3 Lime Avenue.
Woman:	Who lives at 5 Lime Avenue?
Man:	Mr. Hill.
Woman:	And at 7 Lime Avenue?
Man:	Mr. Mendez's sister lives at 7 Lime Avenue.
Woman:	Who lives at 9 Lime Avenue?
Man:	Tom.
Woman:	And who lives at 2 Lime Avenue?
Man:	Jenny.
Woman:	What about 4 Lime Avenue? Who lives at 4 Lime Avenue?

Man: Mr. Cooper.
Woman: And at 8 Lime Avenue?
Man: Mr. King.
Woman: Oh! And I know Ben lives at 6 Lime Avenue.
Man: That's right.

Write the names of the people who live in the street on the board: *Miss Fisher, Mr. Green, Tom, Jenny, Ben, Mr. Cooper, Mr. Hill, Mr. Mendez's sister, Mr. King.* Pupils write the names in their exercise books. Play the cassette again, pausing after each piece of information, and ask pupils to write the correct house number next to each name in their books.

Key

Miss Fisher **1**
Mr. Green **3**
Tom **9**
Jenny **2**
Ben **6**
Mr. Cooper **4**
Mr. Hill **5**
Mr. Mendez's sister **7**
Mr. King **8**

Play the model dialog on cassette and practice the question and answer: *Who lives at number 2?* *(Jenny.)*, with the class. Then in pairs, pupils ask about the other houses in the street.

AB 26 ex A Who lives here? Write sentences.

- Look at the pictures with the class. Ask: *Who are these story characters?* Pupils, on their own or in pairs, work out which character lives in each house, then write sentences about them.

- Check the answers with the class by pointing to each picture and asking: *Who lives here?*

Key

1 Cinderella lives here.
2 Willow lives here.
3 Red Riding Hood lives here.
4 Mr. Wolf lives here.
5 Mrs. Little lives here.

Ending the lesson

- Sing the song *Can you color a rainbow?* (Unit 8).

44

Lesson 2

> **Language**
>
> *Addresses:*
> *(Jenny) lives at (2) Lime Avenue.
> *I live at (1) Lime Avenue.
> *This is his (car).
> *This is her (cat).
>
> **Materials needed**
>
> drawing materials

* = *new language*

Beginning the lesson

- Write the "house numbers" *1* to *10* on pieces of card. Give the pupils the "house numbers". Ask: *Who lives at 3 Lime Avenue?* (pupil raises card). Say: *(Maria) lives at 3 Lime Avenue. Who lives at 5 Lime Avenue?* Pupils say: *(Carlos) lives at 5 Lime Avenue.*

- The cards could also be stuck on the board with pupils' names written behind them. Pupils must guess who lives at each number.

PB 36 ex 2 Where do they live?

Talk to your friend.

- Discuss the envelopes on page 36 of the Pupils' Book. Teach the new word *address*. Say: *Point to Tom's address,* etc.

 Play the model sentence on cassette.

- In pairs, pupils make sentences about the addresses.

Key

Tom lives at 9 Lime Avenue.
Jenny lives at 2 Lime Avenue.
Miss Fisher lives at 1 Lime Avenue.
Mr. Green lives at 3 Lime Avenue.
Ben lives at 6 Lime Avenue.

 Pupils write their own addresses. Teach *I live at …* . Then help pupils to say their addresses. Longer numbers are usually said as single digits; for example, 223 is said as two-two-three. Pupils may need help with numbers such as 23 (twenty-three) or 100 (one hundred). For this exercise, just teach individual pupils the numbers they need.

AB 26 ex B Write sentences with *his* or *her*.

- Pupils find the owners of the items in the pictures by following the lines, then write sentences with *his* or *her*: *This is his hat*, etc.

- Check the answers. Point to the pictures and ask: *Whose hat is this? (This is her hat.)*

Ending the lesson

- Pupils draw the street or area where they live, and then talk about their pictures with their friends. Go around the class asking questions: *Who lives here? Whose house is this?*

- Keep the pupils' drawing for the next lesson.

Lesson 3

> **Language**
>
> Is it a (bird)?
> Who lives at (2) Main Street?
>
> **Materials needed**
>
> counters, spinners or dice

Beginning the lesson

- Ask pupils questions about their drawings from Lesson 2: *Is this your house, (Maria)? Who lives here?* etc.

PB 37 ex 3 Is it a ...?

Game.

- Explain the game to the pupils in L1. They should play in pairs with a spinner or a die, and a counter for each pupil.

A spinner

- Each pupil must throw or spin a 6 to begin. Then they move forward the number of squares that they spin. When they land on a square with a question they must answer it. If the answer to the question is *yes* they can move forward three spaces, and if it is *no* they must move backwards two spaces.

- Help pupils to read the questions and answer them.

- Pupils who finish early can play the game again, perhaps making up their own questions.

AB 27 ex C Write the questions.

- Pupils look at the picture and write the questions to go with the answers.

  Key

  1 Who lives at 5 Main Street?
  2 Who lives at 2 Main Street?
  3 Who lives at 1 Main Street?
  4 Who lives at 4 Main Street?
  5 Who lives at 3 Main Street?

- Pupils practice the questions and answers in pairs. They can also color in the houses and talk about them: *Miss Bell's house is blue*, etc.

AB 27 ex D Write the addresses on the envelopes.

- Pupils look at how Debbie Smith's address is written on the first envelope. They write Peter Green's address on the second envelope and their own address on the third.

  Key

  > Peter Green
  > 7 Forest Street
  > Seaport, Maine
  > 04101

Ending the lesson

 Sing the song *Can you color a rainbow?* (Unit 8).

Lesson 4

Language

Is this your (house)?
Who lives here?
This is (Ben).
My name's (Jenny).
I live at (2) Lime Avenue.

Materials needed

drawing materials

Beginning the lesson

- Ask pupils questions about where they live: *Where do you live, Maria? Who lives in your house?* (*My mother, my father and my brother.*)

- Pupils can ask each other.

 Write the story.

- Discuss the story. Ask questions in English: *Who lives in this house?* (*Willow.*) *Whose car is this?* (*Willow's.*)

- On their own, or in pairs, pupils write the words in the story.

  Key

  Thomas: Is this your house?
  Mr. Wolf: No.
  Thomas: *Who* lives here?
  Mr. Wolf: *Willow* the witch.
  Look! This is her *car*.
  And this is *Willow*.
  Willow: Ha! Ha!

- Pupils form groups of three and act out the story. They could also perform it with the puppets and puppet theater.

 Listen. Write the numbers on the envelopes.

Play the cassette. Pupils listen and write the numbers on the letters.

Tapescript and key

My name's Mr. Brown. I live at 7 Elm Street.
My name's Mrs. Allen. I live at 10 Elm Street.
My name's Peter Green. I live at 2 Elm Street.
My name's John Smith. I live at 5 Elm Street.
My name's Mary White. I live at 8 Elm Street.

- Check the answers with the whole class. Ask questions: *Who lives at 7 Elm Street?* (*Mr. Brown.*)

Ending the lesson

- As a group activity, pupils draw a street with houses, and the people who live in them. Pupils work in pairs, each pair drawing a different house in the street.

- Pupils talk about their houses and the people who live in them: *This is 1 Elm Street. Mr. Green lives here. This is his car. It's green. This is his cat and this is his dog.* They could also write labels to stick on the street next to each house.

Assessment activity

- Ask pupils to draw a picture of a house where someone they know lives.

- Pupils ask and answer about the pictures, e.g. *Who lives here? My grandmother (lives here).* They can then write about their pictures.

Unit 10 A spider in the bathroom

Background information

Mary hates spiders. She has found a spider in the bathtub and screams for help. The rest of the family rush to find out what is the matter.

Lesson 1

Language	New words and expressions
It's (small)/It isn't (big).	big
*There's a (spider) in	small
the (bathroom).	spider
This is the (kitchen).	bee
*in	*Rooms in a house.*
*I like (spiders).	hall
*I don't like (ants).	living rooom
	kitchen
	bathroom
	bedroom
	Help!
	Come quickly!
	Take it away!
	Give it to me!
	There it is!
	Where?
	back yard

Materials needed

drawing materials for exercise 1

* = *new language*

Beginning the lesson

- Ask pupils questions about themselves: *What's your name? How old are you? What's your address?*

- Use pictures in Pupils' Book to ask questions: *Is this a dog? Is this a car? Is this a house? Whose house is this?*, etc.

PB 38/39 A spider in the bathroom

Listen and look.

- Open Pupils' Books at page 38 and discuss the story in L1. Where is this? (Ben and Mary's house.) What is happening? Which room is Mary in? How does she feel?

- Teach the key word *spider*.

 Listen to the cassette. Pupils follow the story in the Pupils' Book.

- Teach the new words *bathroom, big, small, like, don't like*.

- Talk about the story in English. Say: *Point to the bathroom. Point to the spider.* Ask: *Is the spider in the bathroom?* (Yes.) *Who likes spiders?* (Sally.) *Who doesn't like spiders?* (Mary.) *Is the spider big?* (No.) *Is it small?* (Yes.)

 Play the dialog again, pausing for pupils to repeat.

- Ask pupils (L1) what they are afraid of. Point to the pictures in the motif strip and elicit their reactions to each insect.

PB 40 ex 1 Rooms in a house

Listen and point.

- Discuss the picture of the house in exercise 1 on page 40 of the Pupils' Book, in L1. Ask pupils to talk about and identify the rooms in the house in L1.

 Teach the names of the rooms in the house: *hall, living room, kitchen, bathroom, bedroom*.

 Play the cassette. Pupils listen and point to the rooms.

Tapescript and key

This is our house.
This is the hall.
This is the living room.
This is the kitchen.
This is the bathroom.
This is a bedroom.

Play the cassette again. Pupils listen and repeat.

- Write the words on the board.

Write about the pictures.

- Discuss the pictures in L1. What are these rooms? How do you know? Teach the new word *back yard*.

- Pupils write sentences about the rooms in the pictures.

    Key

    1 This is the living room.
    2 This is the hall.
    3 This is the back yard.
    4 This is the kitchen.
    5 This is the bedroom.
    6 This is the bathroom.

- Point to each picture and ask questions: *Is this the bedroom? (No.) Is this the living room? (Yes.)*, etc.

Ending the lesson

Rooms in a house

Draw your house. Talk to your friend.

 Pupils draw their own houses. Ask them to draw their houses so you can see each room, like the one on page 40 of the Pupils' Book.

 Play the model sentences on the cassette. Pupils repeat. Pupils talk about their drawings with their friends. Keep the drawings for the next lesson.

Lesson 2

Language	New words and expressions
There's a (spider) in the (bathroom).	centipede horse snail
Materials needed	
pupils' drawings from Lesson 1	

Beginning the lesson

- Ask questions about the pupils' drawings: *Who lives in this house? Is this the living room? What's this room? Whose bedroom is this?*

- Save the drawings for the assessment activity.

Find the animals!

Look at the house. Say where things are.

 Play the model dialog on cassette and practice the language *There's a ... in the ...* with the whole class.

- In pairs, pupils make sentences about the house picture in exercise 1 on page 40 of the Pupils' Book.

    Key

    There's a dog in the hall.
    There's a bird in the living room.
    There's a bee in the kitchen.
    There's a spider in the bathroom.
    There's a cat in a bedroom.

    Game: Guess the room.

- Pupils can use the picture on page 40 of the Pupils' Book to play *Guess the room.* One pupil makes a noise like a dog. The other pupils look at the picture and respond *It's the hall.*

Draw the animals in the pictures.

- Pupils read the sentences and draw the animals in the pictures of rooms in exercise A.

Ending the lesson

Game: Noises.

Use noises for things that pupils know the words for in English: *dog, cat, bee, watch (tick, tock), horse.* Then say: *There's a bee in the back yard.* Pupils make the appropriate noise and point to a picture of the back yard. Later, pupils can take turns to make the sentences: *There's a ... in the ... .*

Lesson 3

Language	New words and expressions
I like (spiders).	ant
I don't like (spiders).	
Do you like (spiders)?	

Beginning the lesson

- Play the *Noises game* from Lesson 2.

PB 41 ex 3 | I like spiders

Talk to your friend.

- Practice *I like ...* and *I don't like ...* . Say: *I like cats. I don't like spiders.* Ask pupils to identify the animals in the picture in exercise 3. Teach the new words *ant* and *centipede*.

- Play the model dialog on cassette. Pupils listen and repeat, and then talk about the pictures in pairs.

- Ask questions about the pictures. *Do you like spiders Maria? (Yes.) Do you like ants, Carlos? (No.) Who likes spiders?* (Pupils raise hands) etc.

AB 30 ex C | Find the words. Write the rooms in the house and the animals in the spider.

- Pupils work in pairs to unscramble the letters to make words and write them in the appropriate place.

- Check the answers with the whole class.

  Key

  In the house: hall, bathroom, bedroom, kitchen, living room
  In the spider: ant, centipede, snail, bee, spider

- Pupils can add these words to their picture dictionaries.

AB 30 ex D | Big or small? Write sentences.

- Pupils look at the pictures and say what's in each picture.

- Teach the key words *big* and *small*. Pupils write under each picture: *It's a big ...* and *It's a small ... .*

- Check the answers with the class.

  Key

  It's a big spider. It's a small spider.
  It's a small house. It's a big house.
  It's a small car. It's a big car.
  It's a big dog. It's a small dog.

Ending the lesson

- Talk to pupils about likes and dislikes. *What do you like, Carlos? (I like dogs and cats.),* etc.

Lesson 4

Language	New words and expressions
Do you like (spiders)?	couch
on	wall

Beginning the lesson

- Play the *Noises game* again.

PB 41 ex 4 | A spider in the bathroom.

Song.

- Teach the song. Tell pupils the meaning of *on my slice of bread*. Use the picture on page 41 of the Pupils Book to explain. Ask pupils to name the other animals in the picture.

- Pupils sing the song together. Divide into groups to sing alternate verses. Pupils mime the animals as they sing.

AB 31 ex E | Write the story.

- Discuss what is happening in the story in L1. Then teach the new words *couch* and *on* to describe where the centipede is in the picture.

- Pupils, in pairs, write the missing words in the story.

- Check the answers with the whole class.

Key

Mr. Wolf: Help! *Help!*
RRH: What is it, *Mr. Wolf?*
Mr. Wolf: There's a centipede on my *couch!*
RRH: It's a *big* centipede.
Mr. Wolf: Take it away! I *don't* like *centipedes.*

 Listen. Write ✓ for *like* and ✗ for *don't like.*

Play the cassette. Pupils listen and put a check or a put an x in the spaces.

Tapescript

RRH: Do you like centipedes, Mr. Wolf?
Mr. Wolf: No, I don't like centipedes. Do you?
RRH: Yes, I like centipedes. I like snails, too. Do you like snails?
Mr. Wolf: Yes.
RRH: Do you like cats and dogs, Mr. Wolf?
Mr. Wolf: No! I don't like cats and I don't like dogs!
RRH: I like cats and dogs.
Mr. Wolf: Do you like spiders?
RRH: Yes. Do you like spiders?
Mr. Wolf: Ugh! No.
RRH: I like birthday cakes.
Mr. Wolf: I like birthday cakes, too. Do you like presents?
RRH: Yes.
Mr. Wolf: Oh. Here's a present from me!
RRH: Thank you very much, Mr. Wolf.

- Check the answers with the class:

Key

	Mr. Wolf	Red Riding Hood
centipedes	✗	✓
snails	✓	✓
cats	✗	✓
dogs	✗	✓
spiders	✗	✓
birthday cakes	✓	✓
presents		✓

- Pupils talk with their friends about their own likes and dislikes: *Do you like centipedes?*, etc.

Ending the lesson

Sing the song *A spider in the bathroom* again.

Assessment activity

- Use pupils' drawings from Lesson 1. Tell pupils to draw an animal in each of the rooms in their houses. Pupils tell you about the animals in their houses: *There's a cat in the living room*, etc. Ask questions about the animals: *Do you like cats?*

- Pupils can also write sentences about their drawings: *There's a bird in the bedroom. I like birds*, etc.

Project idea

- Pupils could collect pictures of houses from different historical periods or from different parts of the world. Additional vocabulary should be provided to help them write sentences about the houses.

Unit 11 I like snails

Background information

Tom and Jenny have drawn pictures, showing the things that they like.

Lesson 1

Language	New words and expressions
Who likes (spiders)?	butterfly
I like (snails).	flower
There is	
*There isn't	
*There are	
Whose (hat) is it?	
some	

* = *new language*

Beginning the lesson

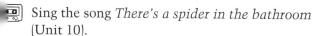 Sing the song *There's a spider in the bathroom* (Unit 10).

PB 42 I like snails

Listen and look.

- Teach the new words *butterfly* and *flower*.

- Listen to the cassette. Pupils follow in the Pupils' Book.

- Ask questions: *Who likes butterflies? Who likes planes? Who likes cats?*, etc.

- Play the cassette again, pausing for pupils to repeat.

- Point to the pictures in the motif strip and ask pupils to tell you what else Tom and Jenny have drawn.

PB 42 ex 1 Which picture is it?

Listen and point.

- Teach *there isn't* and *there are*. Say: *There's a snail in Tom's picture. There isn't a snail in Jenny's picture. There are some flowers in Jenny's picture.*

- Play the cassette. Pupils listen and point to the correct picture.

Tapescript and key

Man: Whose picture is it? There's a dog in this picture. And ... er ... there's a spider in the picture, too. There's a house in the picture. Point to the house. There are some flowers and some trees. There isn't a car in this picture. (Jenny's picture.)

Woman: Point to the picture. Whose picture is it? There's a car and a horse in this picture. The horse is very big. There are two butterflies and there's a dog. There isn't a house and there isn't a plane. There's a snail in the picture. (Tom's picture.)

PB 43 ex 2 There's a snail in Tom's picture

Talk about the pictures on page 42.

- Talk about the pictures on page 42 of the Pupils' Book with the pupils. Say: *There's a car in the picture. Whose picture is it? (It's Tom's picture.) There are some flowers in the picture. Whose picture is it? (It's Jenny's.)*, etc.

- Play the model dialog on cassette. Pupils listen and repeat.

- Pupils work in pairs to make sentences about the two pictures.

AB |32 ex A| **Point to the animals.**

- In pairs, pupils find and point to the animals in the pictures.

- Pupils write sentences about what is different in picture 2. Make sure they realize they can use *there is* and *there isn't*. Check the answers with the class.

Key

There isn't a snail in picture 2.
There is a bird in picture 2.
There isn't a centipede in picture 2.
There is a bee in picture 2.

Ending the lesson

- Ask questions: *Do you like spiders?*, etc. Pupils also ask each other.

Lesson 2

> **Language**
>
> There's a (snail).
> There isn't a (flower).
> It isn't a (dog).
> It's a (cat).
> I like (ants)./(Ben) likes (snails).
>
> **Materials needed**
>
> items of clothing

Beginning the lesson

 Sing the song *There's a spider in the bathroom.*

PB |43 ex 3| **What's wrong?**

Look at the pictures and read the sentences.

- Practice *Is it?* and *It isn't*, using clothes. Hold up a sweater and say: *Look! It's a hat!* Then ask: *Is it a hat? (No.)* Say: *It isn't a hat. It's a sweater.*

- Look at the pictures. Ask (L1) what's wrong. (All the animals are behaving strangely. They think they are a different animal.)

- Pupils look at the first picture and read the sentence. Ask: *Is it a horse? (No.) What is it? (It's a dog.)*

 Play the model dialog on cassette. Pupils listen and repeat. Ask pupils to talk about the pictures in pairs.

Key

1 It isn't a horse. It's a dog.
2 It isn't a dog. It's a snail.
3 It isn't a cat. It's a horse.
4 It isn't a spider. It's a bird.
5 It isn't a bird. It's a cat.
6 It isn't a snail. It's a spider.

- Pupils can talk in the same way, pointing to other pictures in the book:

    A: It's a butterfly.
    B: It isn't a butterfly. It's a bird.

AB |32 ex B| **Write sentences with *likes* and *doesn't like*.**

- Talk about the pictures: *Is there a butterfly in the picture? Point to the butterfly.* Pupils point. Ask questions about the girl in the pictures: *Does she like spiders? (No.)* Tell pupils to write sentences about what she *likes* and what she *doesn't like*.

- Check the answers with the class by asking questions: *Does she like spiders?* Write the sentences on the board.

Key

1 She likes flowers.
2 She likes birds.
3 She likes butterflies.
4 She likes bees.
5 She doesn't like spiders.
6 She doesn't like snails.

- Pupils can talk about themselves in the same way. Ask: *Who likes spiders?* Pupils raise hands and the others answer: *(Maria) likes spiders.*

Ending the lesson

Game: I like spiders.

One pupil starts the game by saying: *I like (spiders).* The next person says: *(Maria) likes (spiders) and I like (dogs).* The next says: *(Maria) likes (spiders), (Carlos) likes (dogs) and I like (flowers).* The game continues until a pupil forgets or makes a mistake. Continue playing from the start again.

Lesson 3

Language	New words and expressions
(Ben) likes (horses).	I think ... .
Who likes (snails)?	
I like (ants).	
I don't like (spiders).	
Do you like (dogs)?	
Materials needed	
Drawing materials	

Beginning the lesson

- Play the game *I like spiders* (Unit 10).

 PB 44 ex 4 **What do you like?**

Follow the lines.

- First, ask pupils to guess what the characters in the pictures like. Teach the expression *I think ... (I think Tom likes dogs.)*, etc. Then pupils follow the lines to find out what the different characters like.

- Play the model dialog on cassette. Pupils listen and repeat. In pairs, pupils talk about the pictures.

- Ask questions to check the answers: *Who likes cars? (Tom likes cars.)*

  Key

  Tom likes cars.
  Ben likes spiders.
  Elvis likes butterflies.
  Mary likes books.
  Sally likes presents.
  Jill likes dogs.

- Pupils can use these pictures to talk about their own likes and dislikes: *Do you like cars? (No.) Do you like books? (Yes.)*, etc.

 PB 44 ex 5 **What do you like?**

Draw a picture of the things that you like. Then draw a picture of the things you don't like.

- Pupils draw pictures showing the things they like and the things they don't like.

- Pupils talk about their pictures to their friends. Teach any new words pupils need to use.

AB 33 ex C **Write the story.**

- Discuss the story in L1. Ask pupils to tell you what is happening in the story.

- In pairs, pupils write the dialog to tell the story.

  Key

  Willow: *What's your* name?
  Thomas: Thomas.
  Willow: Do you like my house?
  Thomas: *No./Yes.*
  Willow: There's a *spider* in my kitchen. I like spiders. Do you *like spiders?*
  Thomas: *No.*

- Pupils act out the story in pairs.

Ending the lesson

- Talk to pupils about their pictures:

  Teacher: Tell us about your picture, (Maria).
  Maria: I like horses and cats. I don't like spiders.

- Alternatively, the pictures could be displayed. Pupils guess who drew each picture by asking questions.

  Teacher: Whose picture is this?
  Pupil: I think it's Maria's picture. Do you like butterflies and centipedes, Maria?
  Maria: No. It isn't my picture.

Lesson 4: Activity Lesson

Language
There's a (flower) in the (kitchen).
Materials needed
cardboard, scissors, glue, pencil, poster paint

Beginning the lesson

- Play the game *I like spiders* (Unit 10).

  Listen and draw.

Play the cassette, pausing for pupils to draw. Pupils listen and draw.

Tapescript and key

1 There's a flower in the kitchen.
2 There's a butterfly in the back yard.
3 There's a snail in the bathtub.
4 There's a spider on the bed.

- Check the pupils' answers. Pupils talk about the drawings: *There's a flower in the kitchen*, etc.

- In pairs, pupils could talk about other things to add to the pictures: *There's centipede in the kitchen.*

 Make a house.

- Demonstrate what pupils have to do by making a sample house in front of the class. Say the instructions *cut, fold, stick*, etc. aloud as you make it.

- Pupils make and color their own houses following the instructions in the Activity Book. They can do this in pairs or in groups.

- Talk about pupils' houses: *Whose house is this? What color is your house? (Red and yellow.). Point to the bedroom. Point to the kitchen.*

Ending the lesson

Game: Whose house is this?

- Use the houses made by pupils to play a game: *Whose house is this?* Describe a house. *It's green and yellow. There are some blue flowers in the back yard. Whose house is it? (It's Maria's house.)*

 Sing the song *There's a spider in the bathroom* (Unit 10).

Assessment activity

Class survey: likes and dislikes.

- Pupils make a chart showing things they like and dislike. Pupils ask their partners questions: *Do you like dogs?*, etc. and fill in the chart.

names	🐕	🕷	🐈	🐛	🚗
Monica	✓	✓	✓	✗	✓
Carlos	✓	✗	✗	✗	✓

- You can base questions and answers on the results of the survey: *Does Carlos like dogs? (Yes.) Who likes cats? (Maria.).*

Unit 12 I like pizza

Background information

The Taylor children, Mary, Eddy, Ben and Sally, are being taken to a restaurant by their grandparents. It is a self-service restaurant and the grandparents are helping the children to choose their meals.

Hamburger restaurants and pizza parlors are other common fast-food restaurants.

Lesson 1

Language	New words and expressions
Do you like (pizza)? *What kind of food do you like?	pizza salad fish and fries sandwich burger milk shake egg cheese chips milk yogurt cookies ice cream sausage everything but

* = *new language*

Beginning the lesson

- Practice *like* and *doesn't like* by playing the game: *I like spiders* (Unit 10).

PB `45` **I like pizza**

Listen and look.

- Open Pupils' Books at page 45 and discuss the picture in L1. Ask pupils to compare the food available in the restaurant in the picture to the food they usually eat.

- Teach the key words: *pizza, burger, salad, fish and *fries, sandwiches, milkshake,* using the pictures in the motif strip.
  **fries* are called *chips* in British English. *Fish and chips* is a very popular dish in Britain, and the word *chips* is often used in American English with this dish instead of *fries*.

- Listen to the cassette. Pupils follow the story in the Pupils' Book. Ask pupils to point to the different kinds of food in the picture: *Point to the sandwiches,* etc.

- Teach *everything*. Teach the new expression *What kind of food do you like?* Ask: *What kind of food does Ben like? (Pizza and burgers.)*

- Play the dialog again, pausing for pupils to repeat.

PB `46 ex 1` **What kind of food do they like?**

Listen and point.

- Pupils look at the pictures and then identify the characters and the food.

- Play the cassette. Pupils listen and point.

Tapescript and key

Ben likes pizza.
Grandma likes salad.
Mary likes fish and fries.
Eddy likes burgers.

- Ask questions: *Who likes salad? (Grandma likes salad.),* etc.

- Play the model dialog on cassette. In pairs, pupils talk about the people in the picture.

> **A:** What kind of food does Ben like?
> **B:** He likes pizza.

- Pupils look at the food in the restaurant again and choose what they like.

 PB ⁴⁶ₑₓ₂ **What do you like?**

Talk to your friend.

- Teach the new words *banana, milk, potato chips, egg, cheese, yogurt, ice cream, apple, sausage, cookies* by referring to the picture on page 46 of the Pupils' Book.

- Tell pupils to point to the different kinds of food: *Point to the ice cream*, etc.

- Play the model sentence on cassette. In pairs, pupils talk about the pictures.

Ending the lesson

- Ask pupils questions about themselves and their friends: *Do you like eggs, Maria? (Yes.) Does Carlos like apples? (Yes.)*

Lesson 2

> **Language**
>
> I like (apples) but I don't like (cheese).
>
> **Materials needed**
>
> large sheet of paper and drawing materials for survey

Beginning the lesson

- Ask questions about food: *Do you like cheese?*, etc.

- Pupils make sentences about the things they like and don't like using the pattern: *I like (apples) but I don't like (cheese).*

PB ⁴⁷ₑₓ₃ **Find their food**

Read and match.

- Talk about the pictures. Tell pupils that these are lunch boxes for the Taylor family. Explain that they must read the sentences and then match the lunch boxes to the family members.

- In pairs pupils read the sentences and match them to the numbered boxes. Check the answers.

Key

1   Mary
2   Dad
3   Grandma and grandpa
4   Mom
5   Ben
6   Eddy

AB ³⁵ₑₓ A **Write the names of the foods.**

- Pupils label the pictures by writing the names of the food underneath them.

Key

eggs, banana, apples, fish and fries, cheese, potato chips, pizza, milk, salad, yogurt, burger, cookies.

AB ³⁵ₑₓ B **Find ten kinds of food in the chain.**

- Pupils circle the names of the food in the chain.

Key

banana, ice cream, milk, chips, pizza, apple, eggs, sandwich, sausage.

- Pupils can make a chart to show which foods are most popular. Pupils draw and color pictures of food, or they can use magazine pictures. Each pupil places a star with their name on it beside their favorite food.

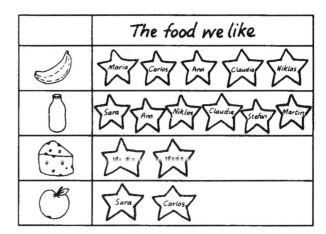

Ending the lesson

Game: Mr. Wolf likes sausages.

The first player says *Mr. Wolf likes sausages.* The second says *Mr. Wolf likes sausages and ice cream.* The third says *Mr. Wolf likes sausages and ice cream and ...,* etc. If a player can't think of anything they are out of the game.

Lesson 3

> **Language**
> (Tom) likes (pizza).
> (I) like (burgers).
>
> **Materials needed**
> Paper for drawing.

Beginning the lesson

- Ask pupils what their favorite food is. Pupils also ask each other.

PB 47 ex 4 **My favorite food!**

Draw a picture of your favorite food. Talk to your friend.

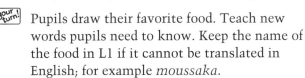 Pupils draw their favorite food. Teach new words pupils need to know. Keep the name of the food in L1 if it cannot be translated in English; for example *moussaka.*

- Pupils talk to their friends.

    A: My favorite food is burgers. What's your favorite food?
    B: Pizza.

AB 36 ex C **Write sentences with *like* or *likes*.**

- Ask pupils to guess what the characters like: *I think Zap likes burgers,* etc.

- Pupils follow the lines to find out what the characters like and then write sentences. Before they write, practice saying the sentences aloud.

    Key

    1 Stella and Arca like apples.
    2 Felina likes fish and fries.
    3 Zap likes pizzas.

4 Mr. and Mrs. Astra like burgers.
5 Rover likes sausages.

- Practice the questions: *What kind of food does Zap like? (Pizzas.) What kind of food do Stella and Arca like?* Pupils can practice in pairs.

AB 36 ex D **Read and draw.**

- Pupils read the sentences. Pupils draw the food in each child's box and then color their pictures.

- In pairs, pupils practice questions and answers about their pictures: *What kind of food do you like? I like Peter's food,* etc.

Ending the lesson

- Use pupils' drawings from exercise 4. Ask: *Whose picture is this? Guess.*

    Pupil: I think it's Maria's. Do you like salad, Maria?
    Maria: Yes. But I don't like milkshakes. It isn't my picture.
    Pupil: Do you like salad and milkshakes, Carlos?
    Carlos: Yes. It's my picture.

Lesson 4

> | **Language** | **New words and expressions** |
> | --- | --- |
> | Do you like (sandwiches)? | drinks |
> | What do you like? | |
> | I like (snails). | |
> | It's my favorite. | |

Beginning the lesson

- Play the game *Mr. Wolf likes sausages* from lesson 2.

AB 37 ex E **Write the story.**

- Discuss the story in L1. Ask pupils to tell you what they think is happening in the story. (Thomas and Willow the witch are having a picnic. Willow doesn't like any of the food until some snails appear.)

- Pupils write the dialog in pairs.

Key

Thomas: Do you like *sandwiches?*
Willow: No.
Thomas: *Do you like* cookies?
Willow: No.
Thomas: What *do you like?*
Willow: *I like snails.*

- Pupils practice the dialog in pairs.

 What does Sophie like? Listen and check the foods.

 Play the cassette. Pupils listen and check the foods that Sophie likes on the cafe menu.

Tapescript

Woman: Hm. Let's see. What kind of food do you like, Sophie?
Sophie: Erm ... I like fish and fries and I like salad.
Woman: Do you like pizza?
Sophie: No, not much ... Mmm! I like ice cream. It's my favorite!
Woman: What drinks do you like?
Sophie: I like milk.
Woman: A milkshake?
Sophie: No, just milk, thank you.

- Check the answers.

Key

Pupils should check the fish, fries, salad, ice cream and milk.

- Pupils use the menu to talk about the food that they like or don't like.

  A: Do you like burgers?
  B: No, but I like pizza.

Ending the lesson

- Pupils could draw and write their own menus. Or they could make up a menu for Willow the witch with snail sandwiches and centipede pizza, and anything else that they think Willow might like.

Assessment activity

- Pupils write sentences to go with their pictures of their favorite food: *My favorite food is pizza and ice cream.*

Project ideas

- Pupils can draw and write about different foods and where they come from. They could also find out about foods that people eat in different countries.

Unit 13 Where is it?

Background information

Ben, who is very messy, has lost his scarf, so he looks for it all over the house. First he looks in his bedroom, and then in the living room, where he finds it, finally. He realizes that he has now lost his gloves.

Lesson 1

Language	New words and expressions
*Where's (the sock)?	closet
*Where are (the gloves)?	chest
*in/on/under/behind	chair
	door
	cupboard

Beginning the lesson

- Play the game *Mr. Wolf likes sausages* (Unit 12).

PB 48/49 | Where is it?

Listen and look.

- Open Pupils' Books at page 48 and discuss the story in L1. What's happening? Do pupils ever lose things? What do they do when they lose things?

- Ask pupils to compare Ben's room to their own rooms at home.

- Listen to the cassette. Pupils follow the story in the Pupils' Book.

- Teach the words for furniture: *bed, couch, chair, closet, table, bathtub* by referring to the motif strip. Teach *Where's ...* . Ask questions: *Is Ben's scarf in the closet? (No.) Is it under the bed? (No.) Is it in the chest? (No.) Where's Ben's scarf? (It's on the chair. It's under Elvis.)*

- Play the dialog again, pausing for pupils to repeat.

PB 50 ex 1 | Where's Mozart?

Listen and point.

- Tell pupils that Mozart likes hiding. They have to find him in each picture.

- Teach the new word *cupboard*.

- Play the cassette. Pupils listen and point to the pictures.

  Tapescript and key

  Where's Mozart?
  He's under the bed. (1)
  Now he's in the cupboard. (4)
  Look! He's on the couch. (3)
  And now he's behind the door. (2)

- Pupils ask questions about the pictures in pairs: *Where's Mozart? He's under the bed*, etc.

AB 38 ex A | Read and draw.

- Identify the furniture in the pictures. Say *Point to the chair. Point to the couch*, etc.

- Pupils, working on their own or in pairs, read the sentences and draw the things in the right places.

- Check the answers. Ask questions: *Where's Willow's cat? It's in the cupboard*, etc.

Ending the lesson

- Give pupils an object and tell them to put it in different parts of the classroom: *Maria, please put my glove under the table. Where's the glove, Carlos?* etc.

- After some practice, pupils tell each other to put the object in different places and ask questions.

- Pupils can add furniture words to their picture dictionaries.

Lesson 2

Language	New words and expressions
Where's (my book)? in/on/under/behind	head

Beginning the lesson

- Ask questions about objects in the classroom: *Where's my book? It's on the table. Where's my scarf? It's on your chair*, etc.

- You could hide objects, such as pieces of fruit, in the classroom before the lesson for pupils to find.

PB 50 ex 2 | **Find the clothes!**

Look at the picture. Answer the questions.

- Review the names of clothes with the pictures in the Pupils' Book Unit 6 (page 22) or with the clothes pupils are wearing.

- In pairs, pupils read the questions and find the clothes in the picture. Make sure they see the difference between the singular and plural clothes.

- Check the answers with the whole class.

  Key

  Ben's scarf is on the chair. (It's under Elvis.)
  Mary's hat is behind the couch.
  Mrs. Taylor's jacket is behind the door.
  Sally's sweater is on her head.
  Mr. Taylor's socks are under the couch.
  Eddy's shoes are behind the chair.
  Ben's gloves are on the sofa.
  Mary's T-shirts are in the cupboard.

 Play the model dialog on cassette. Pupils repeat.

- Pupils practice the questions and answers in pairs.

AB 38 ex B | **Write the answers.**

- In pairs, pupils read the questions and write the answers.

  Key

  1 They're under the chair.
  2 They're on the flowers.
  3 It's in the cupboard.
  4 They're on the table.
  5 It's under the bed.
  6 It's behind the door.

- Pupils can color the picture and then ask questions about it: *What color is the table? What color are the apples?* etc.

- Pupils, in pairs, can ask each other to draw other objects in the picture.

  A: Draw a centipede under the table.
  B: *(draws centipede)* Draw a banana on the cupboard.

Ending the lesson

Game: Show me.

- Describe something in the classroom using words pupils know: *It's big. It's blue. It's under my table. What is it? Show me.* Pupil points to teacher's bag.

- After some practice, pupils can play this game in pairs.

Lesson 3

Language
Where's (my hat)? Where are (my shoes)? It's (under the couch). They are (on the bed). Whose?

Beginning the lesson

- Play the game *Show me*.

My bright red hat!

Song.

 Introduce the song and practice it in the usual way.

- Divide the class into two groups. One group sings questions and the other group sings the answers. Pupils could substitute other items of clothing for *hat*.

 Write the story.

- Discuss the story in L1. What is Willow looking for in each picture? Where does she find the spider?

- In pairs, pupils write the story. Check the stories with the whole class.

Key

Willow: Where are my gloves?
Thomas: They're *on the chair.*
Willow: *Where's* my book?
Thomas: *It's under the couch.*
Willow: *Where are* my shoes?
Thomas: *They're behind the cupboard.*
Willow: *Where's* my spider?
Thomas: *It's on your hat!*

- Ask questions about the story. *Where are Willow's gloves? (They're on the chair.)*

- Pupils, in pairs, act out the story.

 Listen and draw a line.

Play the cassette. Pupils listen and draw lines from the children to their shoes.

Tapescript and key

Where's Sophie's shoe?
It's under the couch.
Where's Claire's shoe?
It's in the chest.
Where's Robert's shoe?
It's on the couch.
Where's Lee's shoe?
It's on the chair.
Where's Peter's shoe?
It's on the cupboard.

- Check the answers with the class by asking questions: *Where's Sophie's shoe? It's under the couch*, etc.

- Pupils can ask questions in pairs: *Whose shoe is under the couch? (Sophie's.)*

Ending the lesson

- Sing the song *My bright red hat!* again.

Lesson 4: Activity Lesson

Language	New words and expressions
Where's the (cat)?	bend
It's (in the chest).	circle
They are (on the chair).	
Whose?	
Is this your favorite (hat)?	
Materials needed	
cardboard, string, scissors, glue, poster paint	

Beginning the lesson

- Sing the song *My bright red hat!*

 Where's the cat?

Game.

- Explain the game to the pupils. Each pair of pupils uses a spinner for this game. One pupil spins for a question: *Where's the cat?* and the second spins for an answer: *It's in the closet.*

Play the model dialog on cassette. Pupils repeat.

- Demonstrate the game with a couple of pupils to make sure everyone has understood. Pupils continue playing in pairs.

- Pupils can draw some examples such as the socks on the bed.

AB [40 ex E] **Make a witch's hat.**

- Pupils can make one hat each, or work in pairs. Pupils draw and cut out the shapes and stick them together as shown in the pictures.

- Before the lesson make a pattern for the hat so it will be the right size. The large circle should have a diameter of about 12 inches and the quarter circle should have a radius of about 12 inches.

- Talk about the finished hats: *Whose hat is this? Is this your favorite hat? Whose hat do you like?*

Ending the lesson

Game: Where's the witch's hat?

 Use one of the hats made by pupils (or another object if pupils haven't made hats). Play the song *My bright red hat!* on cassette. Pupils pass the hat around the class. Stop the music. Pupils ask: *Where's the witch's hat?* The pupil with the hat puts it somewhere, for example under their chair and answers the question: *It's under my chair.* Start the music again and continue in the same way.

Assessment activity

- Put five or six objects in the different places in the classroom to illustrate *in, on, under* and *behind*. Tell pupils to ask and answer questions orally: *Where's (the apple)? It's under the chair.* Then ask them to write sentences: *The apple is under the chair*, etc.

Project idea

- Pupils, in groups, can cut out and collect magazine pictures of furniture. Each group collects furniture for a different room, for example, kitchen, living room, bedroom. Their pictures could be displayed as a poster, with the different items of furniture labeled.

Unit 14 A safari park

Background information

The Taylor family are visiting a safari park. Visitors to the park can drive around and see wild animals in "natural" surroundings. The Taylor family arrive by car. Everyone is wearing seat belts because in America seat belts are compulsory for all car passengers. They are given guides to the park at the gate where they pay to enter the park. The children dream about mixing with the animals, but in fact they must stay in the car with the windows closed because many of the animals are dangerous.

Lesson I

Language	New words and expressions
we	safari park
There are	lion
*Are there any (seals)?	crocodile
*No, there aren't.	elephant
*How many (seals) are there?	tiger
	seal
I love (tigers).	monkey
	baby
	I don't know.
	Look over there!
	Here you are!

* = *new language*

Beginning the lesson

- Play the game *Where's the witch's hat?* (Unit 13).

- Count from *1* to *10* round the class. Tell pupils to count the number of times you clap your hands (first slowly and then faster) or the number of objects you hold up or put on a table.

 **A safari park**

Listen and look.

- Open Pupils' Books at page 52 and discuss the story in L1. Explain what a safari park is, if necessary. Ask pupils to look at the pictures in the motif strip and tell you (L1) what kind of animals they could see in a safari park (wild animals). Ask pupils to identify the people and the animals in the pictures.

 Listen to the cassette. Pupils follow the story in the Pupils' Book.

- Teach *Are there any ...?* and *How many ...?* Ask questions about the story: *Who likes lions?* (*Sally.*) *Are there any lions in the safari park?* (*Yes.*) *How many lions are there?* (*Six.*) *Who likes crocodiles?* (*Ben.*) *How many children are there in the car?* (*Three.*)

 Play the dialog again, pausing for pupils to repeat.

PB 54 ex I Are there any seals?

Listen and point to the animals.

- Teach the names of the animals in the picture on page 54 of the Pupils' Book: *elephant, monkey, tiger, seal, crocodile.*

Play the cassette. Pupils listen and point. Pause the cassette for pupils to find the animals.

Tapescript and key

Ben: Are there any crocodiles?
Mary: No there aren't.
Ben: Oh. Are there any elephants?
Mary: Yes. There are three elephants. There are two big elephants and a baby elephant.
Ben: Great! Are there any tigers?
Mary: Yes, there are two tigers.
Ben: And lions?
Mary: Yes, there are six lions.
Ben: Are there any monkeys?
Mary: Mm. Yes, there are. There are five monkeys.
Ben: Are there any seals?
Mary: Seals? Yes, there are four seals.
Ben: And look over there! There are some birds.
Mary: Yes, there are one, two, three, four, five six, seven birds!

- Talk about the pictures. Point to the lions. *How many lions are there?* (*Six.*) Point to the elephants. *How many elephants are there?* (*Three.*) Point to the baby elephant. *How many baby elephants are there?* (*One.*)

AB 41 ex A **Write the names of the animals.**

- Pupils write the names of the animals beside their enclosures. Check the answers with the whole class.

  Key

  monkeys, tigers, elephants, crocodiles, seals, lions.

Ending the lesson

- Ask pupils about animals: *Do you like lions?* (*Yes.*) *What kind of animals do you like?* (*Tigers.*)

- Pupils conduct a class survey about the animals they like. Pupils' answers could be presented as a bar chart.

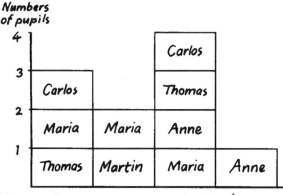

The animals we like

Lesson 2

Language

Are there any (seals)?
How many (seals) are there?
There are (five).

Materials needed

drawing materials

Beginning the lesson

- Ask pupils to name as many animals as they can.

PB 54 ex 1 **Are there any seals?**

Talk to your friend.

In pairs, pupils talk about animals, following the model dialog on cassette. They should ask questions about the animals shown on the left, and answer them by looking at the picture of the safari park.

PB 55 ex 2 **Ten fat monkeys!**

Song.

Introduce the song in the usual way.

- Pupils can do actions with the song by holding up fingers to show the number of monkeys in the song.

- Pupils could also act out the song, with one pupil being the lion and other being the monkeys.

AB 41 ex B **Write questions and answers about the animals.**

- Pupils look at the pictures and write questions and answers about the picture in exercise A.

  Key

  1 How many lions are there? Six.
  2 How many monkeys are there? Eight.
  3 How many tigers are there? Two.
  4 How many seals are there? Five.
  5 How many crocodiles are there? Four.
  6 How many elephants are there? Three.

Ending the lesson

- Pupils draw their own safari parks, including their favorite animals.

- This could be a class activity. Groups of pupils draw different animals, to make a large picture for the classroom wall. Groups could also write about their animals: *There are six elephants. We like elephants. They are big.*

Lesson 3

Language	New words and expressions
This is	pet
His/her name is (Pobby).	
He/she is (three) years old.	
He/she likes (salad).	

Beginning the lesson

- Talk to pupils about their pictures of safari parks: *Are there any lions in your safari park, Carlos?* (Yes.) *How many lions are there?* (Five.)

 PB 55 ex 3 **Pets**

Read and match.

- Pupils read about the pets and match them to the pictures. Check the answers with the class and ask questions: *What's the dog's name?* (*His name is Pobby.*) *How old is he?* (*He is three years old.*) *What does he like?* (*He likes sausages.*)

Key

1	Pobby the dog.	2	Roo the horse.
3	Tabby the cat.	4	Budgie the bird.

AB 42 ex C **Write about the pictures.**

- Ask pupils to look at the pictures and tell what animals they can see. Ask: *Are they in a safari park?* (No.) *Where are they?* (In a house.).

- In pairs, pupils write sentences about the pictures. Check the answers with the whole class.

Key

1 There are three elephants in the kitchen.
2 There is one/a lion in the bathtub.
3 There are four monkeys behind the door.
4 There is one/a seal on the bed.
5 There are five dogs on the couch.
6 There are two crocodiles under the bed.
7 There is one/a bird on the table.
8 There are two tigers in the back yard.

- Pupils ask questions about the pictures: *How many elephants are there in the kitchen?*, etc.

- On small cards write different animal names: *tiger, monkey, elephant, lion, crocodile.* Make sure there is one card for each pupil. Give the cards out in random order. Then divide the classroom into four sections: *kitchen, bathroom, living room, hall.* Ask questions: *How many tigers are there in the bathroom?* Pupils in the "bathroom" count and answer. After some practice, pupils can ask questions themselves.

Ending the lesson

 Sing the song *Ten fat monkeys!*

Lesson 4

Language
What's your favorite (animal)?
Do you like (elephants)?
This is (my pet).
My favorite (color) is/are (red).
Materials needed
drawing materials

Beginning the lesson

 Sing the song *Ten fat monkeys!*

 PB 55 ex 3 **Pets**

Draw your pet. Talk to your friend.

 Pupils draw their pets, either pets they actually have, or pets they wish they had.

- Help pupils to talk about their pets, teaching new words if necessary. E.g. *This is my pet. He's a fish. His name's … .*

AB 43 ex D **Write the story.**

- Discuss the story in L1. (Willow is visiting a safari park, and the keeper is talking to her about the animals. She is frightened of the tigers and a monkey steals her hat.)

- Pupils write the story in pairs. Check the answers.

Key

Thomas: This is the safari park.
Willow: How many tigers *are there*?
Keeper: There are *four*. Do you like *tigers*?
Willow: *No*.
     How *many monkeys are there*?
Keeper: *One*. Do you like *monkeys*?
Willow: *No*.

- Pupils can act out the dialog in pairs. They could also continue it to include other animals.

AB 43 ex E **Listen. What do John and Sophie like? Write the words.**

Play the cassette. Pupils listen and write the words in the table.

Tapescript

Man:	Sophie. What's your favorite animal?
Sophie:	Hm. I think my favorite animals are elephants.
Man:	And what's your favorite food?
Sophie:	Well, I like burgers but my favorite food is ice cream.
Man:	And what's your favorite color?
Sophie:	Red.
Man:	And John. What's your favorite animal?
John:	Well, I like dogs but my favorite animals are horses.
Man:	And what's your favorite food?
John:	Hm ... I know ... pizza!
Man:	And what's your favorite color?
John:	Green.

- Check the answers with the whole class. Ask questions: *What's Sophie's favorite animal? (Elephants.)*, etc.

Key

name	favorite animals	favorite food	favorite color
Sophie	elephants	ice cream	red
John	horses	pizza	green

- Pupils fill in the blanks in the table showing their own favorite animals, food and colors, then talk about it with their friends.

A: What's your favorite animal?
B: (Cats.)
A: What's your favorite food?, *etc.*

- This information could be recorded on a chart, using drawings instead of words.

	favorite animals	favorite food	favorite color
Maria			
Pilar			

- The completed chart can be used for practicing questions and answers: *What's Maria's favorite food? (Pizza.)*, etc.

Ending the lesson

- Pupils can pretend the classroom is a safari park, with different animals in different areas and other pupils as keepers. They can then talk about each area: *The crocodiles live here. There are ten crocodiles.* They can also do a tour of the "safari park": *Look! There are the tigers! How many tigers are there!*

- Other pupils can pretend to be the animals as the keeper introduces them.

Assessment activity

- Pupils draw food on a kitchen table. Ask questions about their drawings: *How many apples are there! (Five.)*, etc. They could also write sentences: *There are five apples on the table. There are two cucumbers*, etc.

Project idea

- Pupils, in groups or as a class, choose a particular animal to find out about: Where does it come from? What does it eat? How does it live in the wild? They collect pictures of their animal.

Unit 15   I'm making a robot!

Background information

Tom and Jill visit Ben and find him making a robot in the living room of his house.

Lesson 1

Language	New words and expressions
This is (his head).	robot
*These are (his legs).	body
*What are you doing?	eye
*I'm ... ing	ear
*He has (a head).	nose
*Give me (the legs).	mouth
	arm
	leg
	neck
	make

* = *new language*

Beginning the lesson

- Sing the song *Ten fat monkeys!* (Unit 14).

PB 56/57   I'm making a robot!

Listen and look.

- Open Pupils' Books at page 56 and discuss the story in L1. Ask them what they think is happening in the picture.

- Teach the key word *robot*.

- Listen to the cassette. Pupils follow the story in the Pupils' Book.

- Teach the parts of the body, using the pictures on pages 56 and 57: *body, head, mouth, nose, ears, eyes, neck, arms, legs.* Ask questions: *What's Ben making? He's making a robot.*

- Play the dialog again, pausing for pupils to repeat.

PB 58 ex 1   A robot!

Listen and point.

- Play the cassette. Pupils listen and point to the parts of the robot's body.

  Tapescript and key

  Tom: Wow! A robot! Look, this is the body.
  Jill: And this is the head.
  Tom: These are the eyes.
  Jill: These are the ears.
  Tom: This is the nose.
  Jill: And this is the mouth.
  Tom: These are the arms.
  Jill: And these are the legs!

- Play the model dialog on cassette. Pupils repeat and then continue talking about the other parts of the robot in the same way.

AB 44 ex A   A jigsaw. Write the words.

- Explain that these are pieces of a jigsaw puzzle. Pupils can work in pairs to identify the individual parts of the body. Pupils guess who is in the jigsaw.

- Check the answers.

  Key

  leg, eye, neck, nose, ear, arm, mouth, head.
  The jigsaw is of Arca, Zap's sister.

- Ask pupils to make sentences: *This is Arca's leg,* etc.

Ending the lesson

- Play *Mr. Wolf says ...* using parts of the body: *Mr. Wolf says touch your nose, point to your head,* etc.

Lesson 2

Language	New words and expressions
He's ... ing	put

Beginning the lesson

- Draw the outline of a robot on the board. Ask pupils to come to the board: *Maria, please draw the robot's head. Now draw his eyes, Carlos*, etc. Then ask questions: *What are these? They're his ears*, etc.

 What's Ben doing?

Read and match.

- Pupils read and match the sentences with the pictures.

- Check the answers aloud with the class: *Look at picture 1. What's he doing? He's drawing the eyes.*

Key

1. He's drawing the eyes.
2. He's drawing the nose.
3. He's drawing the mouth.
4. He's putting the neck on the body.
5. He's putting the head on the neck.
6. He's putting the arms on the body.
7. He's putting the legs on the body.

- Pupils talk about the pictures in pairs.

PB 59 ex 3 **The robot song!**

Introduce *The robot song!* in the usual way.

- Sing the song again with actions.

AB 44 ex D **Write sentences about the giant with *this is* and *these are*.**

- Discuss the picture in L1. Ask pupils to tell you what is happening. (The children have found a giant asleep on the ground.)

- Pupils write sentences about the giant using *this is* or *these are*. Remind them that *this is* is for singular features, e.g. *neck* and *these are* is for plural features, e.g. *ears*.

Key

1. This is his head.
2. This is his nose.
3. This is his mouth.
4. These are his ears.
5. These are his arms.
6. These are his legs.

Ending the lesson

- Play *Mr. Wolf says ... .*

Lesson 3

Language	New words and expressions
I'm a (robot).	monster
My name's (Rodney).	
I live in (a cupboard).	
I have (a cat).	

Beginning the lesson

- Mime making a robot. Ask: *What am I doing? (You're drawing his eyes.)*, etc.

- Pupils can mime making a robot in pairs.

PB 59 ex 3 **Draw a picture of a robot.**

 Pupils draw a picture of a robot and color it in. As they draw, ask questions: *What's this? Is this the head? What color are his eyes? What's your robot's name?* etc.

- Pupils talk about their robots in pairs.

AB 45 ex C **Write the story.**

- Explain that this is a robot that lives in Zap's house.

- Pupils write the story in pairs. Then check the answers with the class.

Key

Rodney: Hello, I'm a *robot*.
My *name* is Rodney.
I live in a *cupboard*.
I have a *cat* and a *dog*.

- Pupils can "interview" Rodney in pairs: *What's your name?* (Rodney.) *Where do you live?* etc.

 AB 45 ex D **Listen. Write the letters.**

- Teach the new word *monster* by referring to the picture.

Play the cassette. Pupils listen and write the letters in the picture.

Tapescript

A
What are you doing?
I'm making a robot.

B
What are you doing?
I'm drawing a monster.

C
What are you doing?
I'm making a house.

D
What are you doing?
I'm drawing a robot.

E
What are you doing?
I'm drawing a flower.

F
What are you doing?
I'm making a monster.

- Check the answers.

Key

(left to right) D, B, A, E, F, C.

- Pupils talk about the picture in pairs.

    A: What's she doing?
    B: She's making a monster.

Ending the lesson

- Draw an outline of the robot's head and body on the board. Ask: *Does he have a head?* (Yes.) *Does he have a mouth?* (No.) *Please draw his mouth, Maria. Does he have any eyes?* (No.), etc. Continue until drawing is complete.

- After some practice, pupils can do this activity in pairs.

Lesson 4: Activity Lesson

Language

What's this?
What are these?
Is this (a head)?
How many?

Materials needed

drawing materials, cardboard boxes and tubes, glue, yogurt carton, comb

Beginning the lesson

- Sing *The robot song!* again.

AB 46 ex E **Make a robot.**

- The class can be divided into groups to make these robots, or one large robot can be made. Identify the parts of the robot's body before putting them together: *What's this?* (showing a box). *It's the robot's head*, etc.

- Talk about the robot or robots: *What's his/her name? How many eyes does he have? How many ears does he have?* etc.

- Pupils write descriptions about their robot: *This is our robot. His name's ... . He has ... . He likes ... . He lives in ... .*

Ending the lesson

- Play *Mr. Wolf says ... .*

Assessment activity

- Pupils draw a picture of a boy or a girl, or use a picture cut out from a magazine. Pupils label their picture: *This is his head; These are his eyes; He has a blue jacket;* etc.

Unit 16 A model village!

Background information

Jill and Ben are making a model village with their toys. Sally is watching. The photos in exercise 1 are from a real model village in Britain.

Lesson 1

Language	New words and expressions
We're making (a model village).	model village
	station
Don't (touch).	train
We have (a house).	soccer field
Is there a (station)?	river
Are there any (houses)?	bridge
	boat
	store
	people
	photos
	lots of
	real
	little
	Oh, no!

Beginning the lesson

• Sing *The robot song!* (Unit 15).

• Talk about pupils' robot pictures or models: *Whose robot is this? Does he have a mouth? Where are his eyes?* etc.

 **A model village!**

Listen and look.

• Open Pupils' Books at page 60 and discuss the story in L1. What do pupils think is happening? What are Jill and Ben making?

• Teach the key words: *village, train, river, bridge* using the motif strip and the pictures in the story. Ask pupils to point to the *train*, the *river* and the *bridge* in the pictures.

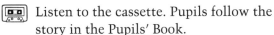 Listen to the cassette. Pupils follow the story in the Pupils' Book.

• Teach *station, soccer field, giant monster, lots of* and *don't touch!* Ask questions about the story: *What are Jill and Ben making? (A model village.) D they have a station? (Yes.) Do they have lots of houses? (Yes.) Do they have a school? (No.) Is there a river? (Yes.) Does Sally have the bridge? (Yes.).*

 Play the dialog again, pausing for pupils to repeat.

 **Is there a station?**

Listen and point.

• Ask pupils (L1) if they have ever been to a real model village. Where was it? Explain that these are photos from a real model village in Britain.

• Teach the new words: *photo, real, boat, store.*

 Play the cassette. Pupils listen and point to the things Mary mentions in the photographs: *river, bridge, boat, houses, stores, people, bus* and *cars.* Pause the cassette for pupils to find the things.

Tapescript and key

Mary: Look, Jill. These are my photos of a real model village in Britain. Look. There's a river and a bridge. And there's a boat on the river. And there are some houses. And look, in this picture there are some stores.

Jill: Are there any people?

Mary: Yes, look, there are some people in the streets.

Jill: Oh, yes. And I can see some cars!

Mary: Yes. And there are some bicycles.

Jill: Is there a station?

Mary: No. I don't think so.

- Talk about the pictures: *Point to the river. What's this, Maria? (It's a boat.) Are there any stores? (Yes.) Show me the stores, Carlos*, etc.

 Play the model dialog on cassette. Pupils talk about the photos in pairs.

Look at the village. Write the letters.

- Pupils look at the picture and match the letters and the words. Check the answers.

Key

station B, bridge D, river C, houses G, school F, soccer field E, train A

- Pupils can ask questions about the picture in pairs:

    A: Is there a school in the picture?
    B: Yes. Here it is.
    A: Is there a bridge?
    B: Yes. Here it is.

Ending the lesson

- In pairs or groups, pupils make model villages, using materials available in the classroom such as pencils, pens, erasers, etc., to represent the different buildings in the village. Talk about their model villages: *What's this? It's the station … and this is the train.*

Lesson 2

Language

Does (Sally) have (a pet)?
What color is (the car)?
There is/There are
Who has my (pencil)?

Materials needed

Boxes of different sizes for model village.

Beginning the lesson

- Make a "model village" at the front of the class with boxes to represent the different parts of the village. Describe the village as you place the boxes: *This is the school. This is the bridge. This*

is a bus, etc. Pupils can guess what the different things are as you make them. When it is finished, ask pupils to point out the different parts of the village: *What's this? (It's the school.)*, etc.

Who are they?

Read and match.

- In pairs, pupils read the descriptions and match them with the pictures.

- Check the answers with the class, and ask questions: *Does Claire have a pet? (Yes, she has a dog.) Does she have a sweater? (No.)*, etc.

Key

1 Nicola   **2** Alex   **3** Claire

 Play the model dialog on the cassette. Pupils talk about the pictures in pairs.

Write sentences about the village. Use *there is* and *there are*.

- Pupils write sentences about the village in the picture in exercise A with *there is* and *there are*. They can use the words they already know. Teach new words they might need, for example: *church, pond, playground*.

- Check pupils' sentences with the whole class.

Key

1   There are two bridges in the village.
2   There's a station in the village.
3   There's a river in the village.
4   There are eight houses in the village.
5   There's a school in the village.
6   There's a soccer field in the village.
7   There's a train in the village.

Ending the lesson

Game: Who has my pencil?

- Take a pencil or another object from one of the pupils. Get the pupil to stand with his or her back to the class. The other pupils pass the object round the class while you play some music on cassette. Stop the music. The pupil holding the object must try to hide it, before its owner turns round. The owner of the object must find out who is holding it: *Who has my pencil? Do you have my pencil, Maria? (No.) Do you have my pencil, Carlos? (Yes.)* It is then Carlos's turn to stand up, and the game continues.

Lesson 3

Language	New words and expressions
I have (a soccer ball). He/she has (a fan).	(In rhyme): bicycle van fan fishing rod roller skates bat pen pal

Beginning the lesson

- Play the game *Who has my pencil?*

PB 63
ex 3 **I have a bicycle**

Rhyme.

- Teach the new words: *bicycle, van, fan, fishing rod, roller skates, bat* by referring to the picture.

 Play the cassette. Pupils listen and read. Play the cassette again. Pupils listen and point to the pictures.

- Pupils recite the rhyme with actions: pedalling a bicycle, driving a van, kicking a soccer ball, fanning oneself, fishing, stroking a cat, roller-skating, flapping wings like a bat.

AB 48
ex C **Write sentences about Cinderella and her sisters. Use *have* and *has*.**

- In pairs, pupils look at the pictures. Then ask questions about the pictures: *Who's this? (Cinderella.) Who has a big bed? (Cinderella's sisters.) Who has lots of cats? (Cinderella.)*, etc.

- Pupils write sentences about the pictures.

Key

1. *The sisters have* a big bed.
2. *Cinderella has* a little bed.
3. *Cinderella has* lots of cats.
4. *The sisters have* lots of hats.
5. *The sisters have* big shoes.
6. *Cinderella has* a small bedroom.

AB 48
ex D **Answer questions about you. Write yes or *no*. Ask your friend.**

- Teach the new word *pen pal*. Pupils read the questions and write *yes* or *no* in the column under *me*. Then they ask their partners questions to fill in the *my friend* column.

- Ask pupils about their answers: *Do you have a dog? (No.) Does (Carlos) have a dog? (Yes.)*

Ending the lesson

- Recite the rhyme *I have a bicycle* again.

Lesson 4

Language
What's this? It's (a soccer ball). I have (a bicycle). We have (a bird).

Beginning the lesson

- Recite the rhyme *I have a bicycle* together, substituting pupils' names for the people in the rhyme:

> **Class:** I have a bicycle,
> (Maria) has a van.
> (Carlos) has a soccer ball ..., etc.

- Pupils could write down their new verse.

PB 63
ex 4 **Do you have an apple?**

Game.

- Pupils play the game in pairs. One chooses a picture, and the other has to find out which picture it is by asking questions.

Play the model dialog on the cassette. Practice the first example with the whole class.

Write the story.

- Ask pupils about the pictures: *Who's this?* (Zap.) *Who's this?* (Zap's friend.) *Where are they?* etc.

- In pairs, pupils look at the pictures and write the story.

   Key

   Zap: This is our village.
   Girl: What's this?
   Zap: It's the *school*.
   Girl: What's *this*?
   Zap: *It's* the *soccer* field.
   Girl: *What's* this?
   Zap: It's the *station*.

- Pupils act out the story. They could extend it to include other features of the village.

Listen. Write the numbers.

- Explain in L1 that these children are at a pet show.

- Play the cassette. Pupils listen and write the numbers beside the people in the picture.

   Tapescript

   1 I have a big dog.
   2 We have a big bird.
   3 I have a cat.
   4 I have three dogs.
   5 We have a mouse.
   6 I have four birds.

- Check the answers.

   Key

   (Left to right) 4, 6, 3, 5, 1, 2.

- Ask pupils questions about the pictures: *Do you have a dog? Do you like birds?* etc. Pupils also ask each other.

Ending the lesson

- Talk to pupils about the area where they live: *Do you have a station? Do you have a soccer field?* etc.

- Ask pupils to draw the area where they live or the area around the school. They label the different buildings, etc. in English, then talk about them to the other pupils.

   A: What's this?
   B: It's the school.
   A: Is there a station?
   B: Yes. Here it is.

Assessment activity

- Copy this picture. Ask pupils to talk and write about it.

Example paragraph

This is my village. It's small. There are two houses in the village. There is a river and a bridge. There is a boat on the river. This is me and my sister!

- An alternative would be to write a paragraph about the village, including lots of mistakes and ask pupils to correct them.

Project idea: Group collage

- Groups or pairs of pupils draw different things which, when put together, make a village or an urban area. They could include new things, for example, supermarkets, gas stations.

Unit 17 We're going to the moon!

Background information

The children are playing a game in the back yard. They have made a pretend spaceship and helmets from household materials. Many houses in America have a back yard. In the middle of big cities, people often live in apartments, where they do not have a back yard.

Lesson 1

Language	New words and expressions
What are you doing?	go
We're going to (the moon).	take off (spaceships)
	walk
our/their	earth
	moon
	helmet
	spaceship
	rocket
	space boots
	astronaut
	Come back.
	Lift off!
	Are you ready?

Beginning the lesson

- Recite the rhyme *I have a bicycle* with actions (Unit 16).

PB 64/65 We're going to the moon!

Listen and look.

- Open Pupils' Books at page 64 and discuss the story in L1. Ask pupils to look at the pictures in the motif strip and tell you what they think the unit is about (space travel). Ask pupils what they think the children are doing. Ask pupils about games they have played with their friends. Have they ever made a spaceship? What else have they made?

- Teach the key words *spaceship* and *moon*.

- Listen to the cassette. Pupils follow the story in the Pupils' Book.

- Teach the new language: *We're going to ...,
sitting, putting on, taking off, helmet, Are you ready?* and *Lift off!* Ask questions about the story: *Where are they going? (To the moon.)
Where are they sitting? (In the spaceship.) What are they putting on? (Their helmets.).*

- Play the dialog again, pausing for pupils to repeat.

PB 66 ex 1 What are they doing?

Listen and point.

- Explain that these pictures show Jill, Tom, Ben and Jenny as real astronauts. Ask pupils (L1) if they would like to go to space.

- Teach the new words: *space boots, rocket, walking, coming back.*

- Play the cassette. Pupils listen and point.

Tapescript and key

Ben's putting on his space boots. (2)
Tom and Jill are putting on their helmets. (1)
The rocket is taking off. (4)
The spaceship is going to the moon. (5)
Ben and Jenny are walking on the moon. (3)
The spaceship is coming back to earth. (6)

- Play the cassette again. Pupils listen and repeat.

- Play the model dialog on cassette. Pupils talk about the pictures in pairs.

> **A:** What are Jill and Tom doing?
> **B:** They are putting on their helmets.

PB 66 ex 2 What's this?

Talk to your friend.

- Play the model dialog on cassette.

- Pupils point to the photos and ask questions about them, using the model in the Pupils' Book.

Ending the lesson

- Play *Mr. Wolf says* .... Include the instructions *stand up, sit down, go to, put on.* (*Put on your hat, scarf, shoes,* etc., can be mimed.)

Lesson 2

> **Language**
> is/are ...ing
> his/her

Beginning the lesson

- Play *Mr. Wolf says* ... .

 Find the words.

- Pupils label the pictures.

- Check the answers with the whole class.

Key

1	spaceship	4	astronaut
2	helmet	5	spacesuit
3	moon	6	earth

AB 50 ex B **Read the sentences. Find the astronauts. Write the letters.**

- Pupils read the sentences and find the people in the picture. Check the answers with the class.

Key

Jenna **B**, Kate **D**, Ken **C**, Mark **A**, Carol and Peter **E**

- Pupils, in pairs, can talk about the picture.

> **A:** Who's this?
> **B:** It's Jenna.
> **A:** What is she doing?
> **B:** She's putting on her helmet.

- Ask pupils to draw a picture of a spaceship preparing to take off. They can then describe to their friends what is happening: *These are the astronauts. They are sitting in their spaceship. This astronaut is putting on his helmet.*

- Keep these pictures for the assessment activity.

Ending the lesson

Game: What am I doing?

- Mime different actions, for example putting on your helmet, taking off your helmet, putting on your space suit, sitting in a spaceship, walking on the moon (moving very slowly). Pupils have to guess the action which is being mimed. After some practice at playing, they can take turns miming and guessing.

Lesson 3

> | **Language** | **New words and expressions** |
> |---|---|
> | They are ... ing. | What's wrong with ...? |
> | doesn't have a/any | |

Beginning the lesson

- Play the game *What am I doing?*

 Flying in a spaceship to the moon

Song.

 Introduce the song and practice it in the usual way.

- Play the song again. Pupils can mime taking off and traveling to space in their rocket.

AB 51 exC **Write the story.**

- Pupils work in pairs to complete the story. Check the answers with the whole class.

Key

Reporter: What are the astronauts doing?
They're *putting on their helmets*.
10–9–8–7–6–5–4–3–2–1 Lift off!
They're *taking off*.

- Pupils act out the story, with some pupils being the astronauts, and others describing what they are doing.

Listen and write the numbers on the robots.

- Explain that the robots in the picture have things wrong with them. Pupils look at the picture and guess what they are.

 Play the cassette. Pupils listen and write the numbers.

Tapescript

Robot number 1 doesn't have a nose.
Robot number 2 doesn't have any arms.
Robot number 3 doesn't have a mouth.
Robot number 4 doesn't have any eyes.
Robot number 5 doesn't have any ears.

Key

From left to right the robots are numbered:
4, 3, 1, 5, 2.

- Check the answers with the class.

- Pupils can talk about the robots in pairs and then write sentences about them.

> **A:** What's wrong with robot number 1?
> **B:** It doesn't have a nose.

Ending the lesson

 Sing the song *Flying in a spaceship to the moon* again.

Lesson 4: Activity Lesson

Language

He hasn't ... .
He doesn't have ... .
His name's ... .

Materials needed

drawing materials
paper, scissors, glue, poster paint,
plastic bottles

Beginning the lesson

- Play the game *What am I doing?*

 A space monster!

Draw a picture of a monster.

- Tell pupils, in L1, to imagine that they meet a monster from another planet. What does the monster look like?

- Play the example text on cassette. Pupils listen, look at the picture and point to the parts of the body as they are mentioned.

Pupils draw and color monsters, and then talk about them to their friends. Go around the class asking questions: *What's your monster's name? Does he have any legs? How many legs does he have?* etc.

 Make a rocket.

- Pupils make rockets in pairs or in groups. Go around the class helping where necessary.

- Ask pupils questions about their rockets: *What color is your rocket? Where is it going?*

Ending the lesson

Sing the song *Flying in a spaceship to the moon*. Pupils can use their rockets to mime taking off, etc.

Assessment activity

- Pupils write sentences about their spaceship pictures: *This is my spaceship. There are three astronauts. They are sitting in the spaceship. They are going to the moon.*

Project idea

- Pupils can find out more about the history of space exploration, copying and labeling pictures from books.

- Alternatively, they could find out about and draw the solar system, naming the other planets.

Unit 18 I'm standing on my head

Background information

The children are doing exercises in the back yard. There is a bird feeder with crumbs and a piece of coconut for the birds.

Lesson 1

Language	New words and expressions
We're ... ing.	exercises
my/our	stand on
Imperatives	touch
(Touch your toes, etc.)	lift
	bend
	toes
	knees
	all together
	jump
	ground

Beginning the lesson

* Sing the song *Flying in a spaceship to the moon* (Unit 17).

PB 68/69 I'm standing on my head

Listen and look.

* Open Pupils' Books at page 68 and discuss the story in L1. What are the children doing? What is Elvis doing?

* Teach the key expression *doing exercises*.

* Listen to the cassette. Pupils follow the story in the Pupils' Book.

* Ask pupils to point to the pictures: *Ben is standing on his head. They're lifting their arms. They're bending their knees. Jill is touching her toes. They are jumping.*

* Play the dialog again, pausing for pupils to repeat.

PB 70 ex 1 What's Jill doing?

Listen and point.

 Play the cassette. Pupils listen and point to the correct picture of Jill.

Tapescript and key

Ben: Look at Jill! She's touching her nose. (1)
Now she's standing on her head. (3)
She's standing on her hands. (5)
She's jumping. (2)
Now she's touching her toes. (4)

 Play the model dialog on cassette. Pupils talk about the pictures in pairs.

AB 53 ex A Write the words in the sentences.

* Teach the new word *ground*. In pairs or alone, pupils look at the pictures and complete the sentences.

* Check the answers with the whole class.

Key

1 They are *doing* their exercises.
2 She's *sitting* on the ground.
3 He's *lifting* his arms.
4 They're *touching* their toes.
5 He's *standing* on his head.
6 They're *jumping*.

Ending the lesson

* Give instructions to pupils: *Touch your toes; Lift your arms; Bend your knees;* etc. After some practice, pupils can give the instructions.

Lesson 2

Language
my/our

Beginning the lesson

- Play *Mr. Wolf says ...* with the new language from Lesson 1. Give pupils a turn to give the instructions.

PB 70 ex 2 | Stand on your head!

Read and match.

- In pairs, pupils read the sentences and match them with the pictures.

- Check the answers with the whole class.

  Key

  1 Stand on your head!
  2 Stand on your hands!
  3 Touch your toes!
  4 Sit on the ground!
  5 Bend your knees!
  6 Touch your nose!

- Pupils talk about the pictures in pairs.

  A: Look at picture 1. What's he doing?
  B: He's standing on his head.

AB 53 ex B | Write sentences with *my* or *our*.

- Pupils look at the pictures and write sentences about them. Make sure they understand why Cinderella's sisters use *our*. (They are thinking about their joint possessions.) Explain the difference between *this is* and *these are*.

- Check the answers with the whole class.

  Key

  1 This is our bed.
  2 These are our hats.
  3 This is our car.
  4 This is my dress.
  5 These are my shoes.

AB 54 ex C | Where are they going?

- Pupils follow the roads to find out where the different characters are going.

- Check the answers orally with the whole class, then pupils write sentences.

Key

1 Mr. Wolf is going to Red Riding Hood's house.
2 Willow is going to the school.
3 Mrs. Little is going to the village.
4 Red Riding Hood is going to Mrs. Little's house.

- In pairs, pupils can talk about the people and where they are going.

  A: Where is Mr. Wolf going?
  B: To Red Riding Hood's house.

Ending the lesson

Game: Where are you going?

- Say: *I'm going to (the station). Where are you going?* The next player says: *You're going to the station and I'm going to (the moon).* Turns to next player: *Where are you going?* Continue around the class in the same way.

Lesson 3

> **Language**
> *Imperatives* (Touch your toes, etc.)

Beginning the lesson

- Play *Where are you going?*

PB 71 ex 3 | Circle

Song.

 Introduce and teach the song in the usual way.

- Pupils can dance to this song following the pictures on page 71 of the Pupils' Book.

AB 55 ex D | Write the story.

- Ask questions about the story in English: *Who's this? What are they doing? Do they like exercises?* etc.

- In pairs, pupils look at the pictures and write the dialog in the story.

- Check the answers with the whole class.

Key

Thomas: Are you ready?
Touch your *toes.*
Touch your *knees.*
Lift *your legs.*
Lift *your arms.*
All together, *jump!*

- Pupils can act out the story in threes.

- Pupils can make sentences by talking and then writing about the pictures: *They are touching their toes; they are touching their knees;* etc.

Ending the lesson

Game.

 Prepare slips of paper with instructions on them: *Touch your toes; lift your arms; take off your shoes;* etc., and put them in a large envelope. Play the *Circle* song on cassette while pupils pass the envelope around the class. Pause the cassette and the pupil holding the envelope takes out a slip, reads the instruction and performs the action. The other pupils must say what he or she is doing: *She's touching her toes,* etc. Start the music again and the game continues until all the actions have been performed.

Lesson 4

Language

She's ... ing
He's ... ing
I'm ... ing
We're ... ing
What is he/she doing?
What are they doing?

Beginning the lesson

- Play the *What am I doing?* game (Unit 17).

PB 71 ex 4 **What's Sally doing?**

Game. Choose a picture.

- Ask pupils to look at the pictures and ask questions in English: *Who's this? (Sally.) Are*

these Sally's shoes? (No.) Whose shoes are they? (Her mother's.), etc.

 Pupils play this game in pairs. One pupil chooses a picture, and the other guesses which picture it is by asking questions. Play the model dialog on the cassette.

- Ask other questions about the pictures: *What is Sally doing in picture 3? She's putting on her hat.*

- Review the words for clothes by telling pupils to mime actions: *Put on your socks! Take off your gloves!* etc. After some practice pupils can give the instructions themselves.

Game: What's different?

- One or two pupils leave the room. While they are out, two or more pupils exchange clothes. When the pupils come back in they must spot what is different and then tell pupils what to do: *Pilar! Take off Maria's sweater!* etc.

AB 55 ex E **Listen. Write the numbers.**

 Play the cassette. Pupils listen and write the numbers.

Tapescript

1 Look! I'm jumping.
2 I'm lifting my arms.
3 I'm bending my knees.
4 We're touching our noses.
5 We're standing on our heads.
6 I'm standing on my hands.

- Check the answers: (left to right) 6, 2, 4, 1, 3, 5

- In pairs, pupils talk about the picture.

   A: What are they doing?
   B: They're touching their noses.

Ending the lesson

- Play *Mr. Wolf says ... .*

Assessment activity

- Do actions and ask: *What am I doing? (You're touching your toes.),* etc.

- Pupils write sentences to go with the picture in exercise E on page 55 of the Activity Book: *They are standing on their heads,* etc.

Unit 19   Mary's pen pal

Background information

In the Taylors' living room, Eddy is watching a pop music program on television and Mary is telling Jill about her pen pal. Mary's pen pal lives in India. Eddy shows a picture of his pen pal, who lives in New York. As he leans over, he accidentally changes the television program to a quiz show.

Lesson 1

Language	New words and expressions
Where does (she) live?	pen pal
How old is (he)?	India
Do they live in (India)?	China
*Numbers 11 – 20	singer
likes	America
doesn't like	right/wrong

* = *new language*

Beginning the lesson

🔊 Sing the song *Circle* with pupils dancing (Unit 18).

- Teach the numbers *11* to *20*. Count up to ten then continue; pupils listen and repeat. Write the numbers on the board in random order and ask pupils to point to them as you say them aloud.

PB 72/73 Mary's pen pal

Listen and look.

- Open Pupils' Books at page 72 and discuss the story in L1. Discuss pen pals and why children have them. Explain that children and adults like to exchange letters with people in their own country and in other countries, though often they have never met their pen pals. Many people find pen pals through advertisements.

- Ask them to guess where Mary's pen pal and Eddy's pen pal come from.

- Teach the key word *pen pal*.

🔊 Listen to the cassette. Pupils follow the story in the Pupils' Book.

- Ask questions about the story: *What's Mary's pen pal's name? (Rani.) Where does she live? (India.) How old is she? (Twelve.) Does Eddy have a pen pal? (Yes.) Where does Eddy's pen pal live? (In New York.).*

🔊 Play the dialog again, pausing for pupils to repeat.

 **AB 56 ex A Who are they? Find and write.**

- Teach the words *singer* and *America*. Explain that the singer in the picture lives in America.

- Pupils follow the lines and find out the names of each of the characters then write sentences.

- Check the answers with the whole class.

Key

Becky is Mr. Wolf's sister.
Boris is Mr. Wolf's brother.
Eric is Mr. Wolf's pen pal
Sharon is Mr. Wolf's favorite singer.

AB 56 ex B Right or wrong? Check the boxes.

- Teach the words *right* and *wrong*. Pupils read the sentences and then check the boxes.

Key

1 right
2 right
3 wrong
4 wrong
5 right
6 wrong

- Ask questions about the people in the pictures: *What's Mr. Wolf's sister's name? (Becky.) Where does Sharon live? (In America.) How old is Mr. Wolf's brother? (Ten.),* etc.

Ending the lesson

- Ask pupils questions about themselves: *Where do you live? Who's your favorite singer? How old are you? Do you have a brother? How old is he? What's his name? Do you like soccer?* etc.

- After some practice, pupils can ask questions. This can be done as a group competition. Divide the class into groups of six to eight pupils. Tell one group to find out as much as they can in two minutes about a pupil in their group by asking questions. Write the answers on the board. The group with the most answers wins.

Lesson 2

Language	New words and expressions
because	beautiful
by	giraffe
with	sport
How many?	soccer team
	on vacation
	dangerous
	brilliant
	Write soon.

Beginning the lesson

- Review counting *1* to *20*. Call numbers out at random and ask pupils to write them down.

 PB 74 ex 1 **Kim and Muridi**

Listen and read. Match the words to the photos.

- Discuss the photos of Kim and Muridi in L1. Ask pupils where they think the children come from. How can they guess?

- Look at the letters from the pen pals. Explain that letters in English begin *Dear ...* . Ask pupils to point to Jenny's pen pal, then to point to Tom's pen pal.

- Play the cassette. Pupils listen and read.

- Teach the new words *giraffe, sport* and *soccer team.*

- Ask questions: *What's Jenny's pen pal's name? (Kim.) Where does Kim live? (In California in the U.S.A.) Does she have any brothers and sisters?*

(Yes.) What are their names? (Shelley and Robert.) How old is Shelley? (Eleven.) How old is Robert? (Thirteen.) Who is Kim's favorite singer? (Bruce Springsteen.) What are her favorite animals? (Dogs.) Does Kim have a dog? (No.) What's Tom's pen pal's name? (Muridi.) How old is he? (Ten.) Where does he live? (Kenya.) What kind of animals are there in Kenya? (Lions, elephants, crocodiles, giraffes.) Is Muridi's village big? (No.) How many sisters does he have? (Four.) Does he have any brothers? (No.) Does he like soccer? (Yes.) What's Muridi's favorite soccer team? (Cameroon.).

- Tell pupils they are going to hear Kim and Muridi talking about the photos. They may not understand every word, but they should still be able to identify the photos and point to them.

- Play the cassette. Pupils listen and point. Pause the cassette when necessary to allow pupils time to find the photos. Note the British English accent as British English is spoken in Kenya. Hence he says football team for soccer team.

Tapescript and key

Kim: This is a photo of my brother and sister. They are on vacation in this picture. They are happy.

This is my cat. She's sitting in the back yard. She likes the back yard.

This is my favorite singer – Bruce Springsteen. I have five tapes by Bruce Springsteen.

Muridi: This is a photo of my village. How many houses can you see?

Here is a picture of my favorite animals – elephants. They are having a bath. Elephants are beautiful, but they can be dangerous, too.

This is the Cameroon football team. They're brilliant.

- Teach the new words *happy, beautiful, dangerous, brilliant.*

- Ask about the photographs. Say: *Point to Kim's brother and sister. Whose cat is this? (Kim's.) Where is it? (In the back yard.) How many tapes by Bruce Springsteen does Kim have? (Five.) Point to Muridi's village. How many houses are there? (Nineteen.) Point to the Cameroon soccer team. Whose favorite soccer team are they? (Muridi's.)*

- Discuss the letters from Kim and Muridi in L1. Ask pupils to think about what they would say to Kim and Muridi in reply to their letters. What else would they like to find out about them and the places where they live? What do they think Kim or Muridi would like to know about their lives?

PB 75 ex 2 **Can you remember?**

Ask your friend questions about Kim and Muridi.

- Ask pupils questions so that they will know what kind of questions to ask: *Who likes soccer? Who has a cat? Where does Kim live? How old is Muridi?*

- Pupils ask and answer questions in pairs. Go around the class helping them to make their questions.

AB 57 ex C **Write the words in the letter.**

- Ask questions about the picture and the letter: *Whose pen pal is this? (Willow's.) What's his name? (Kevin.)*

- Teach the expression *Write soon*.

- In pairs, pupils fill in the gaps in the letter, using words from the box. Check the answers with the whole class.

Key

Dear Willow,
Hello. My *name*'s Kevin. I *live* in the U.S.A. I'm ten *years* old. How *old* are you?
I *like* soccer. My *favorite* food is pizza and salad.
Write soon,
Kevin.

- Ask questions about the letter: *How old is Kevin? (Ten.) What's his favorite sport? (Soccer.) What's his favorite food? (Pizza and salad.).*

Ending the lesson

Game: Who am I?

 Use the information in the letters on page 74 and on the cassette to play a game. Say: *My favorite*

animals are elephants. Who am I? (Muridi.) The first pupil to answer correctly gets the next turn.

Lesson 3

Language	New words and expressions
live/lives	sea
don't	apartment
with	
Materials needed	
Map of the area. Flags or stickers.	

Beginning the lesson

- Play the game *Who am I?* describing pupils in the class this time.

PB 75 ex 3 **Bees live in the back yard**

Rhyme.

 Teach the new words *fish, sea* and *apartment*.

- Teach the rhyme in the usual way. Ask pupils to point to the pictures on page 75 of the Pupils' Book which go with the lines of the rhyme.

- Ask questions using *with*: *Who do you live with? (My mother and father.) Who do you come to school with? (My friend.)*

PB 75 ex 4 **Where do you live?**

Talk to your friends.

- Practice some questions and answers with the whole class: *Where do you live, Maria? What's your address, Carlos?*

Play the model dialog on cassette. Pupils ask each other around the class. Use a copy of a map of the area where pupils live. As pupils answer questions, they can place a flag or a sticker on the map to show where they live.

Listen. Answer the questions.

- Ask pupils to look at the photos and guess information about the pen pals: *Where are they from? How old are they? Do they like soccer?*, etc.

- Play the cassette. Pupils listen and draw circles around the correct answers.

Tapescript

Sophie: This is my pen pal.
Martin: What's his name?
Sophie: Suresh.
Martin: Where does he live?
Sophie: He lives in New Delhi, which is a big city in India.
Martin: How old is he?
Sophie: He's ten.
Martin: What kind of things does he like?
Sophie: Lots of things. He likes sports but he doesn't like soccer. He likes animals and he likes television. Show me your pen pal.
Martin: Here she is. Her name's Yasuko and she lives in Japan. She's nine, the same age as me.
Sophie: Does she have any brothers and sisters?
Martin: Yes, she has two brothers but she doesn't have any sisters.

- Check the answers with the whole class.

Key

1 **a** Suresh **b** India **c** ten **d** no
2 **a** Yasuko **b** Japan **c** nine **d** two

- Ask pupils questions about the pen pals: *Where does Suresh live? What does he like? Does he like television? What's Martin's pen pal's name? How many brothers does she have? Does she have any sisters?*

- Pupils, in pairs, can talk about the children in the pictures.

- Discuss the pen pals in L1. What is Suresh like? What is he wearing in the photo? etc.

Ending the lesson

- Play *Bingo* as in Unit 3 with numbers *1 to 20*.

Lesson 4

Language

What's his/her name?
Where does he/she live?
What color is/are (it)?
What's his/her favorite (animal)?

Materials needed

scissors, colored crayons or poster paint

Beginning the lesson

- Recite the rhyme *Bees live in the garden* again.

 Pen pals!

Draw a picture of your pen pal.

 If pupils do not have a pen pal they could draw a picture of an imaginary one.

- In pairs, pupils can talk about their pen pals.

    A: What's her name?
    B: Caroline.
    A: Where does she live?
    B: In America.

- Pupils can also write about the people they have drawn: *This is my pen pal. Her name is Caroline. She lives in America. She has one brother and one sister. She likes ...,* etc.

 Dress Peter.

- Pupils color and cut out Peter the monster and his clothes. If you don't want pupils to cut the picture from their books you should make photocopies of this page.

- Pupils talk about Peter in pairs.

    A: How old is he?
    B: Ten.
    A: What color are his pants?
    B: Blue.
    A: What's his favorite food?
    B: Ice cream.

- Pupils can make different clothes for Peter, for example a spacesuit.

Ending the lesson

- Play the game *Who am I?*

Assessment activity

- Ask pupils to write a letter about themselves to an imaginary pen pal. As a model, use the letter to Willow in exercise C on page 57 of the Activity Book. Pupils substitute true information about themselves.

Project idea

- Ask pupils to find Kim's and Muridi's countries on a map of the world. Using the map, ask pupils to choose a country in which they would like to have a pen pal.

- If pupils have pen pals, ask them to bring photos and letters to class for the others to see and ask questions about.

- Find out how pupils could get pen pals either in their own country or abroad.

- Pupils can write to "Ben" at Longman! Address letters to:
  "Ben Taylor"
  c/o Longman ELT – Primary publisher
  Longman Group UK Limited
  Longman House
  Burnt Mill
  Harlow
  Essex CM20 2JE
  United Kingdom

Unit 20 Smile please!

Background information

The children are in the park, and Eddy is taking photos with his new camera. The pictures of the park include a duck pond. In the first picture of the story, a woman is feeding the ducks.

Lesson 1

Language	New words and expressions
What are you doing?	make
This is (my camera).	camera
These are (my photos).	new
What's this?	very good
Who's this?	take photos
Whose (head) is this?	Smile please!
	Look at ...

Beginning the lesson

- Recite the rhyme *Bees live in the garden* (Unit 19).

PB 76/77 **Smile please!**

Listen and look.

- Open Pupils' Books at page 76 and discuss the story in L1. Ask pupils to tell you what they think is happening in the story and where they think the children are. Talk about the park and ask pupils what they can see in the background.

- Teach the key words *camera* and *take photos.*

- Listen to the cassette. Pupils follow the story in the Pupils' Book.

- Teach the new words *smile, make, new* and *very good.*

- Ask questions about the story: *What does Eddy have? (A new camera.) What's he doing? (Taking photos.) What's this photo? (It's Mozart.) Point to the photo of Eddy's friend. What's Eddy's*

friend's name? (Peter.) What's Peter doing? (He's making a pizza.) Point to the photo of Eddy.

- Play the dialog again, pausing for pupils to repeat.

PB 78 ex 1 **Eddy's photos**

Listen and point.

- Explain (L1) that these are some of Eddy's photos. Ask pupils to look at these and at the ones in picture 6, page 77. Do they think Eddy takes good photos?

- Tell pupils that they are going to hear Eddy, Jill and Mary talking about Eddy's photos, which are on page 78 of the Pupil's Book.

- Play the cassette. Pupils listen and point to the pictures.

Tapescript and key

Eddy: Look at my photos.
Jill: Who's this?
Eddy: This is er ... yes, this is Sally. *(picture 2)*
And this is a photo of ... I know. It's Mary's head. *(picture 3)*
And whose legs are these? Yes, they're Mary's legs. *(picture 4)*
And who's this? Whose shoes are these?
Mary: They're Jill's shoes. *(picture 1)*
Eddy: Yes. It's Jill.

- Pupils talk about the pictures in pairs.

   A: Who's this?
   B: It's Mary.

AB 59 ex A **What are they making? Write sentences.**

- In pairs, pupils follow the lines to find out what the children are making.

- Check answers orally: *What's Sophie making? (A house.)*, etc., before pupils write sentences.

Key

Sophie is making a house.
Joe is making a (birthday) cake.
Martin is making a pizza.
Katie is making a train.
Kevin and Sue are making a robot.

- Pupils can talk about the pictures in pairs.

    A: Who's making a train?
    B: Katie.

Ending the lesson

- Mime an action and ask pupils: *What am I doing? (You're taking a photo.)* Other actions could be making a pizza, opening a book, doing your exercises, walking.

- Ask pupils to bring photos of themselves, their families or friends to the next lesson.

Lesson 2

Language	New words and expressions
*How many (children) can you see?	children
	wear
What is/are (they) wearing?	see
This is (her head).	feet
These are (her eyes).	
Materials needed	
pupils' own photos	

* = *new language*

Beginning the lesson

- Talk about pupils' photos: *Who's this? (It's my brother.) Where is he? What's he doing?* Help pupils with answers, if necessary.

- Pupils talk about their own photos in pairs.

PB 78 ex 2 A photo album

Talk to your friend about the photos.

- Talk about the photos with the whole class. Teach the new word *children*. Say: *Point to the*

monster. Show me the bedroom, etc. Describe the photos using language pupils already know and ask pupils to guess the picture you are describing. *There are some animals in this picture. My favorite food is in this picture*, etc.

- Teach the new questions: *How many ... can you see?* and *What is/are ... wearing?* Ask pupils some questions about the photos.

- Pupils talk about the photos in pairs. Help them with any new vocabulary they may need.

- Pupils could make a class photo album with the photos of themselves that they have brought to class.

AB 60 ex B Write about the photos.

- Teach the new words *foot* and *feet*.

- Pupils work on their own or in pairs to write the sentences. Check the answers.

Key

1 This is my ear.
2 These are my feet.
3 These are my toes.
4 This is my mouth.
5 This is my nose.

AB 60 ex C Write about you.

- Pupils draw pictures of themselves in the space on the left. Or they could stick a small photo there instead. Pupils fill in the details about themselves (name, age, etc.).

- Check their answers, then ask questions: *What's your favorite color? Where do you live?* etc.

- Pupils can then interview each other in pairs. They could play the parts of characters from *Popcorn* (Zap, Willow the witch, Mr. Wolf, etc.) or other favorite characters from books or television.

Ending the lesson

- Play *Mr. Wolf says ...* to review parts of the body: *touch your nose, touch your ears, open your mouth, sit down, lift your feet*, etc.

Lesson 3

> **Language**
>
> What's this?
> What are these?
> Is it (a camera)?
> Are you ...ing?
> Do you live (in China)?
> Where?
> What's your favorite (color)?
> Do you have (a camera)?
>
> **Materials needed**
>
> spinners and counters for the game

Beginning the lesson

- Play *Mr. Wolf says ... .*

PB `79 ex 3` **Game**

- Pupils play the game in groups of four. When a pupil lands on a square with a question, he or she must answer. If the answer is *yes*, the pupil can move forward one square. If the answer is *no*, or the pupil cannot answer it, he or she must move back one square.

- Move around the class helping pupils and checking their answers.

AB `61 ex D` **Write the story.**

- In pairs, pupils write the story. Check the answer with the class.

    Key

Willow:	Hello, Mr. *Wolf.*
Mr. Wolf:	*Hello, Willow.*
Willow:	What's this?
Mr. Wolf:	*It's a camera.*
	These are *my photos.*
Willow:	What are you doing?
Mr. Wolf:	I'm taking *a/your photo.* Smile please!

- Pupils can act out the story in pairs, using the puppets from the back of the book.

Ending the lesson

- In groups, pupils make up questions for a quiz about the book, for example: *How old is Jill? What kind of food does Eddy like? What's Ben's teacher's name?* Tell each group to make up six questions. Help pupils if necessary, and check that questions are fair. Groups ask each other questions and score points for correct answers.

Game: Who is it?

- Describe a pupil in the class. For example: *Her favorite food is ice cream. She's ... years old. She has a red sweater. Who is she?* Pupils have to guess the name of the pupil.

Preparation for lesson 4

- Prepare cards with the questions from the game on page 79 of the Pupils' Book written on them. You can add extra questions.

Lesson 4

> **New words and expressions**
>
> hair
>
> **Materials needed**
>
> Write the questions from the game on page 79 of the Pupils' Book on separate cards.

Beginning the lesson

 Use cards with questions from the game on page 79 of the Pupils' Book. Put the questions in a large envelope. Play one of the songs on the cassette while pupils pass the envelope round the class. Stop the music. The pupil holding the envelope draws out a question and answers it. Continue until all the cards have been used.

AB `61 ex E` **Listen. Draw the faces.**

- Teach the new word *hair*.

 Play the cassette. Pupils listen and draw the faces.

Tapescript

Picture number 1 is Zap.
Draw Zap's hair.
Now draw Zap's eyes.
Now draw Zap's nose.
Draw Zap's mouth.
And draw Zap's ears. Good!

Picture number 2 is Willow.
Draw Willow's nose.
Now draw her eyes.
Draw Willow's mouth.
Now draw Willow's hair. Her hair is black.
Draw Willow's hat.
And ... er ... oh, yes! Draw Willow's ears. Good!

• Ask pupils to color their pictures and then vote for the pupils who have drawn the best likenesses.

Ending the lesson

• In pairs, pupils choose one of the stories in the Activity Book to act out.

 Sing a selection of the pupils' favorite songs from the cassette.

Assessment activity

• Write the following answers on the board, and ask pupils to make up questions to go with them.

1 I'm ten years old.
2 Fine, thanks.
3 I'm making a pizza.
4 They are in the bedroom.
5 It's blue.
6 I like monkeys and giraffes.

Key

1 How old are you?
2 How are you today?
3 What are you doing/making?
4 Where are (my shoes)?
5 What color is (the sky)?
6 What (kind of) animals do you like?

New words and expressions

Unit 1
hello/hi
good morning
goodbye/bye
thank you/thanks
make

Unit 3
children
please
cut
draw
stick
paint
How do you do?
Be quiet!

Unit 4
house
Come in.
friend
sister
brother
father
grandfather
grandmother
grandpa
grandma
mother
Mom
Dad
dog
cat

Unit 5
picture
bird
plane
school
car
bus
too
I see
ship
train
horse
rat
hen
help!
listen!
dog
cat

Unit 6
hat
I don't know.
That's right!
jacket

T-shirt
skirt
scarf
sweater
dress
coat
glove
shoe
Pick it up.
Look at
socks
Let's go out to play
It's time for bed

Unit 7
Happy birthday!
present
watch
purse
Thank you very much.
Here's your present.
fold

Unit 8
blue
yellow
red
orange
green
brown
black
white
pink
purple
truck
the sky
pants
bananas
lemons
apples
cucumbers
face
oranges
Oh dear!
witch
favorite
gray
rainbow
sun
sea
tree
jeans
eyes
summer
skies
true

Unit 9
street
lives
number
Look!
telephone booth
bus stop
mailbox

Unit 10
spider
bathroom
Help!
Come quickly!
big/small
Take it away!
Give it to me!
kitchen
hall
bedroom
living room
back yard
snail
horse
bee
centipede
ant
couch
wall

Unit 11
butterfly
flower

Unit 12
pizza
burger
salad
fish
fries
sandwich
milk
milkshake
sausage
chips
yogurt
everything
cookies
egg
ice cream
cheese
but
drinks

Unit 13
chair
chest
door

head
closet
cupboard
bend
circle

Unit 14
safari park
baby
lion
crocodile
elephant
monkey
tiger
seal
pet

Unit 15
robot
body
make
mouth
nose
ear
eye
neck
arm
leg
put
monster

Unit 16
model village
station
train
soccer field
river
bridge
lots of
pen pal
bicycle
van
boat
fan
fishing rod
roller skates
bat
store
people
photos
real
little

Unit 17
moon
spaceship
helmet
Are you ready?

Lift off!
rocket
earth
astronaut
go
walk
space boots

Unit 18
exercises
toes
knees
bend
jump
ground
touch
lift

Unit 19
pen pal
India
China
America
singer
right/wrong
beautiful
giraffe
sport
soccer team
on vacation
dangerous
brilliant
sea
apartment

Unit 20
Smile please!
take photos
new
camera
make
children
wear
see
feet
hair

Your name

A How old are they? Listen and write the ages.

1 Lucy   nine   **2** Martin [ ]   **3** Claire [ ]

4 Robert [ ]   **5** Piara [ ]   **6** Steven [ ]

5 points

B Answer some questions about yourself.

1 What's your name? _____

2 How old are you? _____

3 How are you today? _____

3 points

C Read and write the names of Lucy's family.

Hi. My name's Lucy. This is my family.
This is my mother. Her name's Susan.
This is my father. His name's Peter.
This is my sister. Her name's Sarah.
And this is my brother. His name's Robert.
My grandmother's name is Ethel and my grandfather's name is Francis.
And this is Dylan. He's my dog.

7 points

D Answer the questions.

1

Is it a plane?

No, it's a bird.

2

Is it a glove?

_____

3

Is it a house?

_____

4

Is it a bus?

_____

5

Is it a dress?

_____

6

Is it a T-shirt?

_____

10 points

E Finish the questions. Follow the lines. Write the answers.

1 Whose ____**hat**____ is this?

It's Martin's hat.

2 Whose _____ is this?

_____

3 Whose _____ is this?

_____

4 Whose _____ is this?

_____

5 Whose _____ is this?

_____

6 Whose _____ is this?

_____

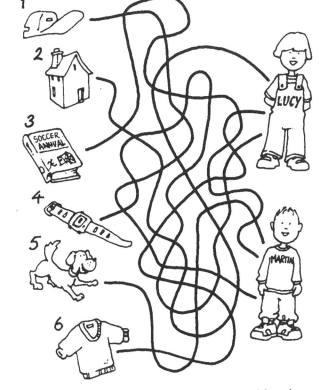

10 points

Your name_____

A Listen to your teacher and color the pictures.

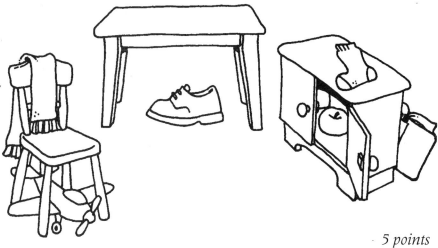

5 points

Answer the questions.

1 Where's the apple?   **It's in the cupboard.**_____

2 Where's the shoe?   _____

3 Where's the book?   _____

4 Where's the scarf?   _____

5 Where's the sock?   _____

6 Where's the plane?   _____

10 points

B Look at the chart. Write sentences.

name	✓	✗	name	✓	✗
Maria	pizza	milk	Sophie	ice cream	eggs
George	apples	fish	Claire	cup	hamburgers
John	sandwiches	bananas	Martin	pasta	salad

1 **Maria likes pizza but she doesn't like milk.**_____

2 _____

3 _____

4 _____

5 _____

6 _____

10 points

C Write the names of the rooms.

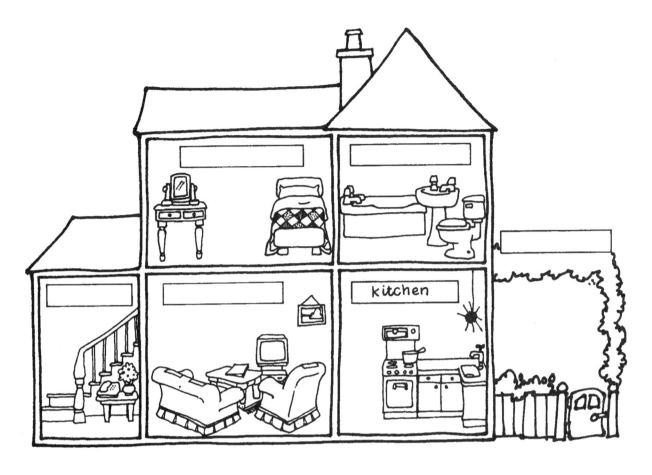

5 points

Read and draw the animals in the house.

This is my house. There's a big spider in the kitchen.
There's a bird in the living room. There's a dog in the
bedroom. It's a small dog. There's a cat in the hall.
There's a horse in the back yard.

10 points

D Match the questions and answers.

What color is the sky?	Yes, there are five.
What's your favorite color?	Jenny.
Are there any horses?	I like pizza.
Who lives here?	Pink.
What kind of food do you like?	There are three.
How many tigers are there?	It's blue.

5 points

Your name_____

A How many does Martin have? Listen and write the numbers.

2

5 points

B Look at the robot. Write the parts of the body.

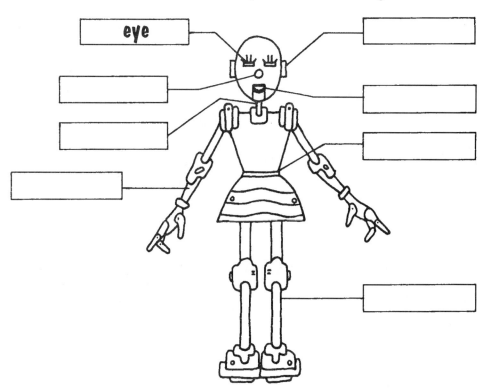

eye

7 points

C Read the conversation. Write *this* or *these*.

A: Look! Do you like my robot? Her name's Automata.

B: Yes. She's very good. What's __**this**__?

A: It's her head. Look, _____ are her eyes, _____ is her mouth and _____ is her nose.

B: What are _____?

A: They're her arms. And _____ are her legs.

B: Oh, yes!

5 points

D What are they doing? Write questions and answers.

1

<u>**What's he doing?**</u>
<u>**He's making a**</u>
<u>**pizza.**</u>

2

_____
_____
_____

3

_____
_____
_____

4

_____
_____
_____

5

_____
_____
_____

6

_____
_____
_____

10 points

E Look at the village.
Circle the right answers.

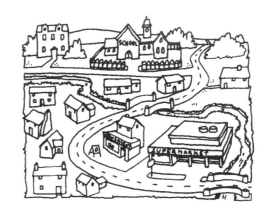

This is my village. It's big/small.
There are ten/twelve houses and
four/two stores. There is/isn't a
station. There is/isn't a river.
There is/are two bridges over the
river. There is/are a school.

6 points

F Fill in the questionnaire. Write sentences.

CONFIDENTIAL FILE   TOP SECRET

○ name: _____

○ age: _____

○ address: _____

   favorite color: _____

○ favorite food: _____

   favorite animal: _____

7 points

Notes on tests and key

Materials needed for tests

Pupils will need a pen, pencil and an eraser. For test 2, exercise A they also need red, brown, yellow, green, blue and black colored pencils.

Teacher's scripts

Exercise A in each test is a listening exercise. Read the script twice: the first time pausing between each sentence and the second time straight through for pupils to check their answers.

Test 1 exercise A
1   Lucy is nine years old.
2   Martin is ten years old.
3   His sister's name is Claire. She's six years old.
4   Robert is eight years old.
5   His sister's name is Piara. She's five years old.
6   His dog's name is Steven. He's three years old.

Test 2 exercise A
The apple is red.
The shoe is brown.
The scarf is yellow.
The sock is green.
The book is blue.
The plane is black.

Test 3 exercise A
These are Martin's toys. He has lots of toys. Look! He has two spaceships (*pause*) and four toy astronauts (*pause*). He has one toy giraffe (*pause*). He has nine cars (*pause*). He has five soccer balls (*pause*). He has one camera (*pause*). The camera is his favorite toy.

Key

Test I

A

1	nine	2	ten	3	six
4	eight	5	five	6	three

C

D
1   No, it's a bird.
2   No, it's a sock.
3   No, it's a school.
4   No, it's a car.
5   No, it's a skirt.
6   No, it's a sweater.

E
1   Whose *hat* is this?
    It's Martin's hat.
2   Whose *house* is this?
    It's Lucy's house.
3   Whose *book* is this?
    It's Martin's book.
4   Whose *watch* is this?
    It's Lucy's watch.
5   Whose *dog* is this?
    It's Martin's dog.
6   Whose *sweater* is this?
    It's Lucy's sweater.

Test 2

A
1   It's in the cupboard.
2   It's under the table.
3   It's behind the cupboard.
4   It's on the chair.
5   It's on the cupboard.
6   It's under the chair.

B
1   Maria likes pizza but she doesn't like milk.
2   George likes apples but he doesn't like fish.
3   John likes sandwiches but he doesn't like bananas.
4   Sophie likes ice cream but she doesn't like eggs.
5   Claire likes yogurt but she doesn't like burgers.
6   Martin likes sausages but he doesn't like salad.